Inside Inequality in the Arab
Republic of Egypt

A WORLD BANK STUDY

Inside Inequality in the Arab Republic of Egypt

Facts and Perceptions across People, Time, and Space

Paolo Verme, Branko Milanovic, Sherine Al-Shawarby, Sahar El Tawila, May Gadallah, and Enas Ali A.El-Majeed

THE WORLD BANK
Washington, D.C.

ISBN (paper): 978-1-4648-0198-3
ISBN (electronic): 978-1-4648-0199-0
DOI: 10.1596/978-1-4648-0198-3

Cover photo: © Andrew Shenouda/Photos.com
Cover design: Debra Naylor, Naylor Design, Inc.

Library of Congress Cataloging-in-Publication Data has been requested

Contents

Box

Figures

Tables

Foreword

Inequality is more fashionable than it used to be. After almost three decades of increasing economic disparities in their own country, US economists and politicians have recently begun to challenge the century-old American belief that inequality does not matter, and to ask uncomfortable questions about both its causes and consequences, including on the link between inequality of incomes and of opportunity. This is not an exclusively American phenomenon: Recent research suggests that the income share accruing to the richest 1 percent of households has been rising in many other places—including a number of European countries generally thought to be rather egalitarian.

Inequality can also be fashionable for the converse reason: in Latin America, after rising or remaining stable for as long as data have been available, inequality fell substantially in the 2000s, in a movement that was both consistent across most (but not all) countries in the region, and persistent for at least a decade. Elsewhere, there is growing concern that high inequality in a number of countries in central and southern Africa may be a factor in explaining why poverty reduction remains sluggish, despite rapid economic growth.

So when the Arab Spring took sudden and dramatic hold of North Africa in 2011, many pointed to high and rising inequality as one of the causes. There was only one problem: Income inequality, as conventionally measured, was *not* high in the region. And in Egypt, its pivotal country, it actually declined in the decade preceding the 2011 revolution—even as the public concern with inequality and injustice were growing.

What was really going on with the distribution of income in Egypt? Was the household survey data wrong? Did other factors account for a rising perception of inequity? How was prosperity—and its growth—shared across the country's disparate regions? How were people in Egypt's poorest villages affected by these dynamics?

These are the questions addressed by this impressive volume, probably the most comprehensive account of income distribution in Egypt for some time. Motivated by the apparent paradox of falls in measured inequality coexisting with growing public concern, the book is the scholarly equivalent of a crime mystery, with its superb team of authors playing the role of detectives.

The authors do not ignore the light others have shed on the question before them, and the first chapter provides a very useful historical survey of the literature on Egyptian inequality. They also avoid the trap of believing that all answers can be found in the computers and archives of the capital city: The book's final chapter contains a fascinating study of 141 among Egypt's poorest thousand villages. In between, chapters 2 and 3 provide the bulk of the painstaking sleuth work on the puzzling discordance between fact and perception of Egypt's inequality in the decade preceding the Arab Spring.

I very much enjoyed serving as a reviewer for the early phases of this work, and came to see it as an example of best practice in distributional analysis at the World Bank. But the completed work is more than that: I believe it is—and will remain for some time—a key reference for anyone interested in income inequality in Egypt. I hope you will enjoy reading it as much as I did.

Francisco H. G. Ferreira
Chief Economist
Africa Region
The World Bank

Foreword

It is almost impossible to find a single country, now or at an anytime in history, where all citizens of that country enjoyed full equality. Egypt is no exception. Therefore, it is tempting to ask: Why should anyone worry about inequality if it is a fact of life?

Well, there are compelling reasons for worrying about inequality. To begin with, there is a growing body of literature that supports the view that inequality of opportunity accounts for a significant part of inequality of outcomes within and between countries. An Egyptian born to rich and educated parents is privileged over an Egyptian born to poor and uneducated parents. Second, significant levels of inequality could have large negative effects on human welfare and society, especially if inequality is associated, or perceived to be associated, with corruption. Last but not least, it is increasingly recognized that more egalitarian societies grow faster than unequal societies, negating the long-held view that with patience the fruits of development will eventually trickle down. Concern for inequality is therefore justified on ethical and developmental grounds.

In the Egyptian context, the timing for a book on inequality could not have been better. The concern for greater equality is high on the agenda of all Egyptians, especially in the wake of the January 25, 2011, revolution. Measuring the extent of inequality and its root causes is the first step toward bringing about greater social justice.

This book goes a long way to achieve this objective. It provides a comprehensive review of the literature on inequality in Egypt over the last 50 years. It places Egypt's inequality in a global context, with a particular focus on spatial inequality. It offers interesting insights into the gap between facts and perceptions of inequality during the period 2000–09. And it offers a detailed analysis of the drivers of inequality in some of the poorest villages in Egypt.

The value of the book lies both in its novelty as well as its relevance to policy making in Egypt. From the perspective of the current government, the facts and insights offered in different chapters fall on receptive ears as the government is committed not only to activating the economy but also to doing so in a more egalitarian manner. Surely, the process of laying firm foundations for achieving high and sustainable growth in Egypt will take some time. But the good news is that Egypt is now more poised to move in a more inclusive direction: more inclusive political institutions and more inclusive distribution of the benefits from growth.

Ahmed Galal
Minister of Finance
Arab Republic of Egypt

Foreword

The question of inequality can hardly be ignored today. We don't have to look very far to be reminded that not everyone has the same odds to a life of prosperity and well-being. Every day, on my way to work, I can witness the stark contrast of how "life" treats two Egyptian girls of the same age, who we shall call Raghada and Amira. Raghada is from Imbaba, rarely attends school, and sells paper tissues on the 26th of July Street in Zamalek. Amira is from Zamalek, does not have to work to help meet her family's needs, and attends regularly Port Said school. In a world of equal opportunities and shared prosperity, both Raghada and Amira would enjoy the same quality of education and the same job opportunities once they finish school. But that outcome is highly unlikely, unless we try to better understand and respond to factors that lead to inequality.

The issue of inequality has become even more important in the wake of the worldwide social movements generated by the 2008 global financial crisis and in the wake of the social movements that characterized the 2011 Arab spring in the Middle East and North Africa region. The World Bank has traditionally worked on inequality as part of its mandate of reducing poverty by pioneering some of the work on the measurement of inequality and on inequality of opportunities that today is used worldwide by researchers and practitioners alike. But recent events have shown that income inequality and the perception of this inequality by the public are potentially explosive social devices that need to be better understood and managed with care. Research on inequality cannot be confined within the walls of academia but needs to be relevant for the public at large and help policy makers to understand how to approach policies that address inequality.

To respond to these new needs and since 2011, the World Bank has been undertaking a number of studies on inequality in Egypt that looked into the economic geography of inequality, inequality of opportunities, and facts and perceptions of inequality. These studies have started to unveil a number of aspects of inequality that were largely neglected in studies that focused primarily on poverty. It became evident, for example, that inequality across regions and the North and South of Egypt is sharp and complex to bridge, that the dimensions that constitute inequality of opportunities are many and not easily addressed by conventional public policies, and that perceptions of inequality are sometimes more relevant than facts when it comes to social unrest. Taken together, these studies offer a very comprehensive overview of inequality and its various dimensions in today's Egypt.

Moreover, since 2011, the World Bank has launched a number of support programs that focus on aspects closely related to inequality including poverty, exclusion from the job market, and exclusion from social services. For example, the Egypt Labor Intensive Investment Project is expected to create 750,000 job opportunities, especially in the poorest communities of Upper Egypt. The World Bank's support to small and micro enterprises reaches out to those businesses that do not have access to the formal banking sector and provides access to finance for expansion and growth of small business, many of them owned and run by women. These are some examples of measures that could contribute to close the gap between the haves and the haves not.

This book is the final product of the latest of the inequality studies and a courageous effort to dig into one of the most controversial aspects of inequality in Egypt, namely the apparent mismatch between facts and perceptions of inequality. It does so by carefully reviewing 60 years of studies on inequality in Egypt, by deconstructing and interpreting the spatial dimension of inequality, by painstakingly reconstituting figures of inequality using recent household data, by analyzing perceptions of inequality through values surveys, and by determining the factors that drive inequality among the very poor. This book helps us to understand why we should not constrain ourselves to the mere measurement of inequality. Income inequality can be a powerful instrument to better understand the state of an economy, but the perception of inequality can be an equally powerful instrument to measure people's views of economic justice.

These are no small achievements of this book, and they encourage us to be more daring and imaginative in our work. Raghada and Amira deserve to know why they are different and how their differences can be bridged, and these questions cannot be satisfactorily addressed by conducting business as usual.

Hartwig Schafer
Country Director for Egypt, Yemen, and Djibouti
The World Bank

Preface

This book joins four papers on inequality in the Arab Republic of Egypt prepared in the framework of the World Bank 2012–13 Egypt inequality study and it is a joint effort between the World Bank and the Social Contract Center of Egypt.

The first paper prepared by Sherine Al-Shawarby reviews the studies on inequality in Egypt since the 1950s with the double objective of illustrating the importance attributed to inequality through time and of presenting and compare the main published statistics on inequality. To our knowledge, this is the first time that such a comprehensive review is carried out in Egypt.

The second paper prepared by Branko Milanovic turns to the global and spatial dimensions of inequality. The objective here is to put Egypt inequality in the global context and better understand the origin and size of spatial inequalities within Egypt using different forms of measurement across regions and urban and rural areas. The Egyptian society remains deeply divided across space and in terms of welfare and this study unveils some of the hidden features of this inequality.

The third paper prepared by Paolo Verme studies facts and perceptions of inequality during the period 2000–09, the period that preceded the Egyptian revolution. The objective of this part is to provide some initial elements that could explain the apparent mismatch between inequality measured with household surveys and inequality aversion measured by values surveys. No such study has been carried out before in the Middle East and North Africa region and this seemed a particular important and timely topic to address in the light of the unfolding developments in the Arab region.

The fourth paper prepared by Sahar El Tawila, May Gadallah, and Enas Ali A. El-Majeed assesses the state of poverty and inequality among the poorest villages of Egypt using a unique survey conducted in 2009/10 and covering over 10,000 people. The paper attempts to explain the level of inequality in an effort to disentangle those factors that derive from household abilities such as health, education, and employment (household characteristics) from those factors that derive from local opportunities such as the availability of health, education, and economic facilities (village characteristics). This is the first time that such study is conducted in Egypt.

Acknowledgments

The book has been prepared by a team led by Paolo Verme and includes Branko Milanovic and Sherine Al-Shawarby of the World Bank and Sahar El Tawila, May Gadallah, and Enas Ali A. El-Majeed of the Social Contract Center of Egypt. The authors thank the World Bank Country Director, Hartwig Schafer; the Cairo World Bank office for assistance during repeated field missions; Dr. Heba El-Laithy for excellent comments at all stages of the work; and the Central Agency for Public Mobilization and Statistics for providing data, explanations, and useful discussions of results. The authors are also very grateful for comments received from Bernard Funck, Francisco Ferreira, Ruslan Yemtsov, Tara Vishwanath, Caroline Freund, and participants to two workshops on inequality held in March 2012 and May 2013 in Cairo.

Contributors

Sherine Al-Shawarby is currently Deputy Minister for Economic Justice at Egypt's Ministry of Finance and a Professor of Economics in Cairo University, Cairo, Egypt. She worked as a resident Senior Economist at the World Bank office in Cairo between June 2001 and July 2013. She also worked as a consultant to several international, regional, and national organizations. Among them are the WFP, the World Bank, USAID, the Social Fund for Development (SFD), the Center for Economic and Financial Research and Studies (CEFRS), and the Institute of National Planning (INP). Al-Shawarby has published several papers on a wide range of issues in Egypt: exchange rate, trade, inflation, fiscal sustainability, subsidies, poverty, and inequality. She holds a Ph.D. in Economics from Cairo University (Egypt).

Enas Ali A.El-Majeed holds an M.Sc. in Statistics from the Faculty of Economics and Political Science, Cairo University, Egypt. She is the Team Coordinator of the Equitable Development Observatory at the Social Contract Center, a joint project between UNDP and the Cabinet, Egypt. Her research interests are mainly in poverty and social protection.

Sahar El Tawila has a Ph.D. in Statistics from Cairo University and received diplomas from the Office of Population Research at Princeton University and the Institute of Social Research at the University of Michigan. In addition to her academic work in both Cairo University and the American University in Cairo, her main areas of expertise include monitoring and evaluation of policies and development programs, and sampling. She was also a consultant to UNDP, UNICEF, WHO, UNFPA on numerous projects and contributed to a number of Egypt's Human Development Reports. Currently, she is the Director of the Social Contract Center, a joint project between UNDP and the Cabinet, Egypt.

May Gadallah is an Assistant Professor at the Statistics Department, Faculty of Economics and Political Science, Cairo University, Egypt and currently works as Senior Statistical Advisor to the Social Contract Center of Egypt. She holds a Ph.D. in biostatistics from the School of Public Health, University of California, Los Angeles, where she also served as a postdoc. She participated in several labor market and social science studies in Egypt and has written papers on gender, labor market, and epidemiology.

Branko Milanovic is Lead Economist in the World Bank Research Department in the unit dealing with poverty and income inequality and is a professor at the School of Public Policy, University of Maryland, College Park. He was a long-term visiting professor at the School for Advanced International Studies in Washington (1997–2007), and Senior Associate at Carnegie Endowment for International Peace in Washington (2003–05). He is the author of numerous articles on methodology and empirics of global income distribution and effects of globalization. His most recent book, "The Haves and the Have-nots: A Brief and Idiosyncratic History of Global Inequality," published in December 2010, has been translated in seven languages and voted by The Globalist as 2011 Book of the Year.

Paolo Verme is the Senior Poverty Specialist for the North Africa and the Middle East region at the World Bank. A Ph.D. graduate of the London School of Economics, he was Visiting Professor of Public Economics at Bocconi University in Milan (2004–09) and contract Professor of Political Economy at the University of Turin (2003–10) prior to joining the World Bank in 2010. He initiated his career working as a volunteer for an NGO in Africa and between 1995 and 2010 served as an advisor to ministries, multilateral, bilateral, private and nongovernmental organizations on the design, implementation and evaluation of labor market, and social protection policies. His research covers labor markets, income distribution, and the evaluation of welfare reforms and is published in international journals, books, and reports.

Abbreviations

CAPMAS	Central Agency of Public Mobilization and Statistics
CDF	Cumulative Distribution Functions
CI	confidence interval
COICOP	classification of individual consumption according to purpose
CPI	consumer price index
ECES	Egyptian Center for Economic Studies
EU	European Union
FBS	Family Budget Surveys
GDP	gross domestic product
GoE	Government of Egypt
HH	household head
HIECS	Household Income, Expenditure and Consumption Surveys
III	Income Inequality Index
ILO	International Labour Organization
IMF	International Monetary Fund
Ln	natural logarithm
M&E	Monitoring and Evaluation
MDG	Millennium Development Goals
NA GDP	National Accounts gross domestic product
NA HH	National Accounts household head
NGO	nongovernmental organization
OECD	Organisation for Economic Co-operation and Development
OLS	ordinary least squares
PPP	purchasing power parity
PSU	primary sampling unit
TDM	total disparities measures
WVS	World Values Survey
WYD	World Income Distribution

Executive Summary

Press coverage of the Egyptian revolution, both local and international, made frequent use of the word "inequality" to describe one of the factors that generated discontent. During the current transitional phase, two of the themes that are inspiring popular debates and political parties in the making are the questions of social justice and equality. The general perception is that social injustice and a somehow unequal distribution of resources were deep-rooted phenomena under the Mubarak regime and that these factors contributed to explain the eruption of social discontent.

This perception is not only conveyed by media and popular debates but also by intellectuals and academics. The Egyptian Center for Economic Studies (ECES), for example, in a policy note argued that, "Social inequality and inadequate human development coupled with the lack of political reforms have been among the main factors that led to the outbreak of the revolution" (p. 7, ECES, Policy Viewpoint, May 2011). The term "inequality" as used by the press and people in the street is a rather loose term that may be associated with inequalities of various kinds such as economic or social status, access to services and resources, or more opportunities in general.

Indeed, one of the puzzling aspects of this malaise about inequality is that the measurement of monetary inequality in the Arab Republic of Egypt by means of household surveys does not seem to match perceptions. According to both official government figures and the World Bank, the Gini coefficient has been declining throughout the last decade from 36.1 percent in 2000 to 30.7 percent in 2009 (World Bank 2007, 2011). This is an atypical trend for low-income countries that experience rapid growth periods. Egypt has enjoyed a very prolonged growth phase since the late 1980s and between 1996 and 2010 the country enjoyed growth rates above 5 percent including peaks of over 7 percent between 2006 and 2008 (www.cbe.org.eg). And the 2009 inequality figure of 30.7 percent is also a very low figure by regional and international standards.

The purpose of this study is to begin to elucidate this puzzle and provide a better understanding of income inequality in Egypt in its various dimensions. We do this by first reviewing the literature on inequality in Egypt so as to put our study into context and better understand how inequality and the interest for inequality have evolved over the past 60 years. There is a tremendous wealth of studies on inequalities in Egypt and we made an effort to review and make sense of these studies in their respective historical context. We then tried to disentangle the global and spatial dimension of inequality by putting Egypt in its regional and global context and by delving into the complex structure of spatial inequality. This part of the study unveils some interesting features of inequality across areas, regions, and people. Next, we reassessed the facts about income inequality by evaluating the quality of Egyptian data and by reestimating all inequality figures. This analysis is followed by an analysis of inequality perceptions based on values surveys that allows contrasting facts with the perceptions and deriving important leads to the explanation of the facts-perceptions paradox. Last, we look into inequality into the poorest areas of Egypt to understand the nature of inequality among the poor and how low inequality can coexists with high poverty. By better understanding the nature of inequality, this part of the study provides some initial indications on policies that can be effective for poverty reduction. In what follows, we summarize more in detail the findings of each part of the study.

Historical Trends of Inequality

Studies on inequality in Egypt have roughly followed three distinct periods. Early studies focused on land inequalities and the rural sector and were conducted in the background of major land reforms in the 1950s and 1960s. The following period was characterized by studies of inequality across urban and rural areas in line with the period of strong emigration and urbanization flows that characterized the 1970s and 1980s. The 1990s and the most recent decade have seen perhaps a decline in the interest for inequality as growth, liberalization, and privatization of the economy attracted most of the attention and the studies of inequalities that appeared did so mostly in the context of poverty studies (table ES.1).

The review of studies on inequality since the 1950s has been able to pinpoint a number of stylized facts:

- Since 1958/59, the Egyptian income distribution has been relatively egalitarian by the standards of developing countries with a peak of 0.45 in 1990/91 and a dip of 0.31 in 2008/09. In fact, the latest figure published by the Central Agency for Public Mobilization and Support (CAPMAS) in November 2013 puts the Gini coefficient at 0.30, the lowest value ever estimated in Egypt.
- The range in which inequality has fluctuated around this declining trend over the 60 years considered is relatively narrow considering the many drastic changes and shocks that the economy has faced over this long period of time. Due to the marked discrepancy in the estimates of the Gini for household consumption for any given year between different studies, and sometimes even between studies of the same authors, these findings need to be treated with caution but witness great and prolonged interest for the subject of inequality in Egypt.

Table ES.1 Selected Inequality Measures, 1958/59–2008/09

	1958/59	1964/65	1974/75	1977[a]	1982	1990/91	1995/96	1999/2000	2004/05	2008/09
Rural										
Adams	0.34	0.29	0.35		0.34					
Radwan1977	0.373	0.353	0.392							
El-Issay 1982	0.37	0.35	0.35							
Korayem 1994					0.29	0.32				
Korayem 2002						0.283	0.275	0.255		
World Bank 2007, Lower Egypt							0.209	0.211	0.228	
World Bank 2007, Upper Egypt							0.241	0.24	0.247	
World Bank 2011									0.22	0.216
Urban										
El-Issawy 1982	0.4	0.4	0.37							
Korayem 1994					0.32	0.38				
Korayem 2002						0.304	0.326	0.35		
World Bank 2007, Metropolitan							0.36	0.37	0.34	
World Bank 2007, Lower Egypt							0.27	0.257	0.282	
World Bank 2007, Upper Egypt							0.35	0.368	0.372	
World Bank 2011									0.34	0.333
Egypt, Arab Rep.										
El-Issawy 1982	0.42	0.4	0.38							
Kheir-El-Din and El-Laithy 2006						0.446	0.345	0.362	0.32	
World Bank 2007							0.345	0.361	0.32	
World Bank 2011									0.313	0.307
Ahmad 2010								0.345		

Source: World Bank data.
Note: III=Income Inequality Index. See chapter 1 for definitions.
a. Based on the data generated from a survey carried out by the International Labour Organization (ILO) in 1977.

Overall, it is possible to trace the development of the income distribution between subperiods in the last 50 years, but we cannot strictly use the values of these estimates to determine the trend of inequality between 1958/59 and 2008/09. All we can say perhaps is that the flagrant inequalities which characterized rural areas in the 1950s improved in the mid-1960s but most probably fluctuated around the same values during the following decades. Although losses in the income shares of the poorest groups were larger in the urban sector than in the rural sector, and consequently the gains of the richest groups were larger in the urban sector than in the rural sector, it is not clear whether the income distribution has significantly changed, especially during the last decade. This calls for a reassessment of spatial inequality, data quality, and a reconsideration of the measures of welfare and inequality.

Spatial Inequality

Egypt inequality has remained low by international standards and comparable to that of other Middle East and North African countries. Income inequality in Egypt as measured by household surveys revolved around a Gini coefficient of 34 percent between 2005 and 2009.[1] This is similar in level to that of the developed European Organisation for Economic Co-operation and Development (OECD) members. It is significantly lower than income inequality in the United States (which exceeds 40),[2] and is likewise lower than inequality in most countries that are close to Egypt in terms of gross domestic product (GDP) per capita. For example, in 2009, Georgia, Guatemala, and China—countries that, in terms of GDP per capita (measured in purchasing power parities [PPPs] terms), are around Egypt's income level—have higher inequality: Guatemala had an income Gini of 57; Georgia, a consumption Gini of 39; and China, an income Gini of 47 (figure ES.1).

Egypt, however, compares better with other Arab countries for which we have the data. Arab countries are distinguished by relatively low inequality with Gini coefficients ranging between around 33 and 40, and Egypt's inequality is, if anything, in the lowest part of the distribution. Although we cannot be sure about the rankings because the welfare concepts and survey methodologies differ, there is no evidence that Egypt's inequality level is higher than in other Arab countries.

Geographical or horizontal inequalities between urban and rural areas are one of the main contributory factors to overall inequality in many countries of the world (figure ES.2). Egypt is not an exception, although we find that inequalities are not huge by international standards, and that they are even less so if we com-

Figure ES.1 Egyptian Gini within the Global Distribution of Gini, 2008–09

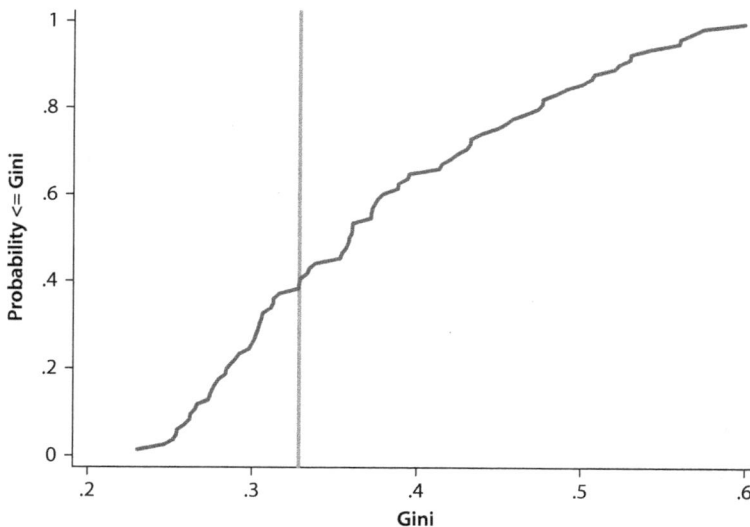

Source: All the Ginis database, HIECS 2009.

Figure ES.2 Distribution of Urban and Rural Gini Coefficients (by Governorate)

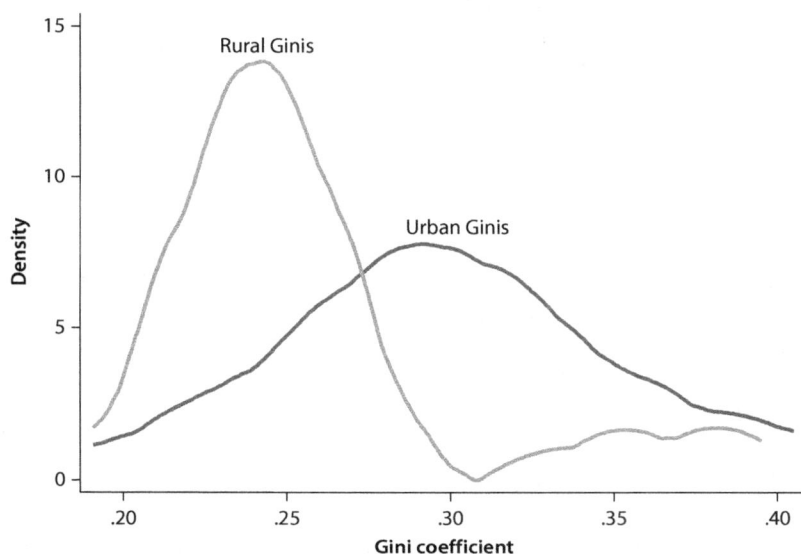

Source: HIECS 2005.

pare urban and rural inequalities within the same governorates. The gap is more geographical, between the four main Egyptian cities, and the rest of the country, than properly urban-rural. Interpersonal inequality in the urban area (as a whole) is significantly greater than interpersonal inequality in the rural area (as a whole).

Similarly, within each governorate, interpersonal inequality in its urban parts (average Gini of about 30) is greater than interpersonal inequality in rural parts (average Gini of 26). This is also not an uncommon feature: Urban incomes tend to be more dispersed reflecting greater variety of population and skills in urban areas. Between 2005 and 2009, the changes in both the urban/rural gap, and inequality have been modest. The urban-rural gap decreased somewhat because the average urban income (as estimated from household surveys) decreased more in real terms than the average rural income. Urban and rural inequalities hardly changed at all. The only notable feature was the divergence across urban governorates' average incomes.

Facts and Perceptions of Inequality

This study researched one of the puzzling aspects of contemporary Egypt, namely the apparent mismatch between income inequality measured by Household Income, Expenditure and Consumption Surveys (HIECS 2000, 2005, 2009) and the perception of income inequality measured by the World Values Surveys (WVSs 2000, 2008). The paper assesses first the quality of the HIECS data by reconstructing welfare aggregates over time and subjecting the data to several tests. It finds that the HIECS data are of good quality, a finding consistent with a more recent study that looked further into the HIECS quality and the measurement of inequality.[3] The paper then finds a number of stylized facts about welfare and inequality in Egypt during the decade that preceded the revolution, which can be summarized as follows:

• Household welfare in real terms has not improved overall between 2000 and 2009 and has declined for most households.
• Poorer households have performed relatively better than richer households between 2000 and 2009 but overall poverty has increased.
• The gap between GDP per capita and household consumption has increased during the last decade. While GDP per capita has grown steadily, household consumption has not increased suggesting that GDP growth has not trickled down to households (figure ES.3).
• Inequality has not increased between 2000 and 2009. The estimated statistics show a decline in the Gini coefficient, which is consistent for income and expenditure and also consistent with previous studies.
• The level of inequality is strongly influenced by richer households. The top 1 percent of richer observed households contributes to inequality more than any other percentile in the distribution and up to 4 percentage points of the gini.
• A missing values analysis shows no evidence of richer households self-selecting themselves out of the sample. A recent study by Hlasny and Verme (2013) largely confirms this finding.

Figure ES.3 GDP, HH Income and Expenditure
Per capita, real terms, 2000=100

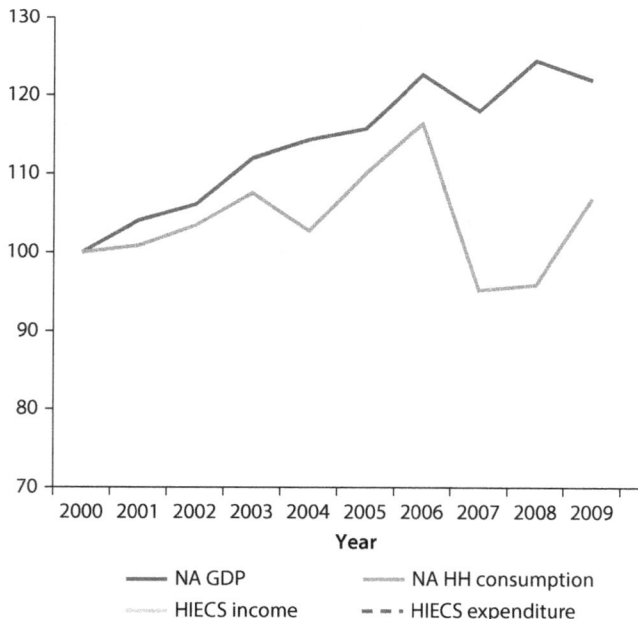

Source: HIECS 200, 2005, and 2009, CAPMAS National Accounts and IMF Economic Outlook database. All data deflated with the IMF CPI inflation rate.
Note: NA GDP = National Accounts gross domestic product; NA HH = National Accounts household head; HIECS = Household Income, Expenditure and Consumption Surveys.

Inside Inequality in the Arab Republic of Egypt • http://dx.doi.org/10.1596/978-1-4648-0198-3

In the light of these facts, how have people's perceptions changed in relation to welfare and income inequality? The paper was able to unveil a number of insights about people's perceptions based on data extracted from the 2000 and 2008 World Values Surveys. The main results can be summarized as follows:

- The 2000–08 period saw a remarkable change in people's perceptions on a vast range of issues. A possible explanation seems to be an increased awareness of the population about economic and social issues and a better sense on the part of households of their own relative position in society.
- People's priorities changed from general views about freedom and the environ-ment to very concrete aspirations about GDP growth and stable food prices.
- There is a clear decline in self-reported incomes and social status. In 2008, households felt poorer than in 2000 and they felt that they belonged to a lower social stratum.
- Between 2000 and 2008, the mismatch between actual welfare and welfare expectations increased.
- There is an evident sharp rise in inequality aversion for almost all income groups and all social groups (figure ES.4).
- Poorer people have grown more inequality averse than richer people despite a relatively better performance over the period.
- Social class is more important than incomes in explaining dislike for income inequality.
- Internationally, there seems to be a negative correlation between the degree of democratization and the growth of dislike for inequality during periods of GDP growth while there is no direct association between GDP growth and inequality aversion.
- Dislike for inequality is also positively associated with freedom and interest in politics and negatively associated with trust and religious practice.

Figure ES.4 Pro-inequality Opinions by Income Deciles, 2000 and 2008

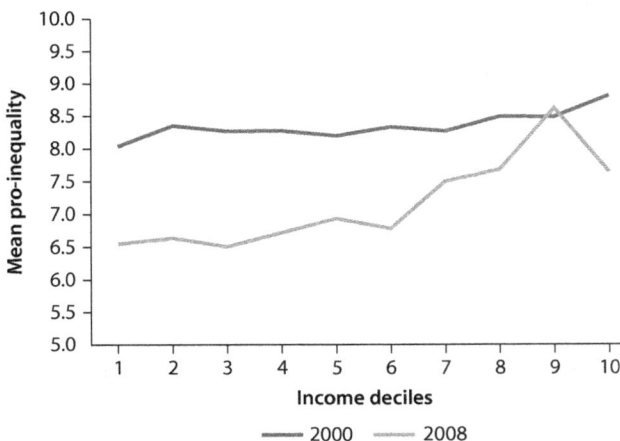

Source: WVS 2000, 2008.

Inside Inequality in the Arab Republic of Egypt • http://dx.doi.org/10.1596/978-1-4648-0198-3

The analysis of facts and perceptions of inequality has largely confirmed the initial puzzle. Income inequality measured with HIECS surveys is effectively low and not a statistical artifact while people have grown more inequality averse. Previous findings on inequality and media reports on perceived inequality are both credible, and the paradox of the mismatch between facts and perceptions of inequality fully stands after our investigation. The question is how to explain the paradox. The paper provided a number of leads that can help to answer this question which can be summarized as follows:

1. *Growth and volatility have changed people's expectations.* Between 2000 and 2009, Egypt has experienced a period of sustained GDP growth and also increased volatility, especially in food and commodity prices. Theory suggests that during such periods people change expectations and this is what we found with the World Values Surveys (WVSs). Egyptians became more worried about issues such as GDP growth and food prices.

2. *People became more socially and economically aware.* We found very significant changes in the distributions of a number of key variables such as life satisfaction, trust, freedom, people's priorities and also inequality aversion. It is as if people became more aware of their relative conditions and expressed this new awareness through changes in views on a broad range of topics.

3. *Absolute household welfare has declined for most households and this resulted in an increased dislike for inequality.* Even if the level of inequality has not increased, Egyptians have increased their dislike for inequality. People can hardly appreciate inequality if their own status and the status of their peers do not improve.

4. *GDP growth has not trickled down to households and this has contributed to the growth of dislike for inequality.* While GDP growth may have filled the pages of newspapers, back home household welfare was not improving as documented by the HIECS. Instead, most of the GDP growth accrued to private enterprises and nongovernmental organizations. This lack of direct gains from growth must have frustrated households and contributed to shape household opinions on income inequality.

5. *The perceived decline in welfare was greater than the actual decline in welfare.* This was documented with the WVS for both incomes and social class and complies with the fact that people became more socially and economically aware.

6. *The mismatch between actual welfare and expected welfare has increased.* This is a natural consequence of the two points above. Egyptians were poorer at the end of the decade as compared to the beginning of the decade but felt even poorer as compared to the actual situation. As suggested by theory, this mismatch is a very strong driver of perceptions about welfare.

7. *Lack of democratic institutions may sharpen adversity to inequality.* We saw that among growing economies less democratic states experienced a sharper growth in inequality aversion. This is not conclusive evidence but an interesting lead for future research.

8. *Change in the reference group*. Social sciences have long ago established the importance of the reference group in determining self-assessed well-being. The reference group is generally defined as the group of people perceived as peers and this is the group that individuals use to compare themselves with others and assess their own status in society. The expansion of Internet-based social networks has clearly changed the reference group in two directions. It has expanded the reference group to encompass a much larger number of people and has broken the national boundaries of the reference group. Through social networks, people gained more peers and peers abroad, across the MENA region and outside the MENA region. By changing the reference group, self-assessed status in society changes and so do expectations and aspirations, which is what we observed in the WVSs. This growth in aspirations and expectations generated by cross-country comparisons in the face of no growth in income or opportunities at home may well explain in part the mismatch between observed inequality and perceived inequality.

While the final culprits of our initial puzzle may not have been found yet, the paper has provided a number of leads to explain the mismatch between facts and perceptions of income inequality. Neither the data nor the people have been found to be wrong. On the contrary, in the light of the evidence provided in this paper we could argue that there is no puzzle and that people's perceptions are fully consistent with the facts if we broaden the analysis to the macro economy and to the behavioral analysis of welfare perceptions.

Poverty and Inequality in Egypt's Poorest Villages

The study assesses for the first time the state of poverty and inequality among the poorest villages of Egypt. For this purpose it uses a unique survey conducted in 2009/10 in 141 among the poorest 1,000 villages of Egypt covering a total of 10.568 households. The poverty rate in these villages is estimated at 81.7 percent against 22 percent for Egypt and 28 percent for rural Egypt, whereas the Gini inequality across households is estimated at 29.4 percent against 31.1 percent for Egypt and 22.4 percent for rural areas. Thus, while the poverty rate in these villages is extremely high, the inequality level is low and very close to the national figure.

The paper attempts to explain the level of inequality using a regression decomposition approach (Fiorio and Jenkins 2007) and a Gini coefficient regression in an effort to disentangle those factors that derive from household abilities such as health, education, and employment (household characteristics) from those factors that derive from local opportunities such as the availability of health, education, and economic facilities (village characteristics).

The paper finds that about 37.3 percent of inequality can be explained by household and village characteristics with the former contributing by 31 percent and the latter by 6.3 percent. However, the factors that contribute to changes in poverty and inequality can have discordant or concordant signs (table ES.2). Only one factor (having a minimum level of education) can reduce both poverty and inequality while factors such as fertility, disability, work in the informal sector outside establishments in agricultural or nonagricultural activities, and male-headed households can increase both poverty and inequality. Factors such as higher employment and higher education which are standard objectives of poverty reduction strategies are found to reduce poverty but increase inequality. Other factors such as government employment and chronic illness reduce inequality but increase poverty.

The results suggest that in the context of Egypt's poorest villages, some of the most significant factors conducive to increased inequality—such as higher employment and higher education—are the same standard objectives of pro-poor poverty reduction strategies. Hence, pro-poor growth accompanied by increased inequality is a legitimate goal that should be pursued. Policies adopted to achieve this goal must also encompass providing incentives to promote investments in areas that are geographically nearby these villages to avail more and better jobs in

Table ES.2 Cross-Classification of the Determinants of Inequality and Poverty Ordered within Cells According to Contribution to Inequality

Ln HH consumption/capita	(+) Contribution (increasing inequality)	(−) Contribution (decreasing inequality)
(+) Coefficient (reducing poverty)	• More are employed among household members • Head of household attained secondary education or higher (especially university or higher) • Ownership of assets (especially agriculture land) • Closer distance to urban centers • More have permanent jobs among employed household members • Having external migrant among household members • Age of head of household is less than 35 years	• Some education
(−) Coefficient (increasing poverty)	• Higher fertility (ratio of children<15 years to household size) • Working in the private sector outside establishment in agriculture • Handicapped among household members • Male-headed households • Age of head of household is 45–55 years • Working in the private sector outside establishment not in agriculture	• Working in government or public sector • Chronic disease among household members

Source: World Bank data.
Note: HH = household head.

private sector establishments. In the context of these poorest villages, ensuring some education, even if it does not lead to completing basic education, remains one main key factor in order to fight extreme poverty while reducing inequality. However, ensuring extended years of education beyond just the basic mandatory stage not only increases the supply of skilled labor but also pays off as it seems to provide diversified opportunities to break out of poverty.

Reducing poverty among the poorest people of Egypt may necessarily entail an increase in inequality and the low level of inequality is explained by the widespread level of poverty rather than by an economy that distribute increasing resources equitably across the population. This is in line with the idea that, at very low levels of incomes, an increase in inequality may signal an improvement in overall living conditions while very low levels of inequality may simply signal widespread poverty.

Notes

1. Note that inequality figures cannot be directly compared across the four chapters in this book because of the different time periods, surveys, welfare aggregates, and measures of inequality used.

2. Note that Gini values are expressed in percentage terms.

3. See Hlasny and Verme (2013).

References

Adams, Richard H., Jr. 1985. "Development and Structural Change in Rural Egypt, 1952–1982." *World Development* 13 (6): 705–23.

———. 1989. "Worker Remittances and Inequality in Rural Egypt." *Economic Development and Cultural Change* 38 (1): 45–71. http://www.jstor.org/stable/1154160.

———. 1991. "The Effects of International Remittances on Poverty, Inequality, and Development in Rural Egypt." Research Report, no. 86, International Food Policy Research Institute, Washington, DC.

———. 2002. "Nonfarm Income, Inequality, and Land in Rural Egypt." *Economic Development and Cultural Change* 50 (2): 339–63. The University of Chicago Press. http://www.jstor.org/stable/10.1086/321913.

Fiorio, C. V., and P. S. Jenkins. 2007. "Regression-based Inequality Decomposition Following Fields 2003." Presentation at Institute for Social & Economic Research (ISER)—University of Essex September. www.stata.com/meeting/13uk/fiorio_ineqrbd_UKSUG07.pdf.

El-Issawy, Ibrahim H. 1982. "Income Distribution and Economic Growth." In *The Political Economy of Income Distribution in Egypt*, edited by Gouda Abdel Khalek and Robert Tignor. New York: Holmes and Meiser Publishers.

Hlasny, V., and P. Verme. 2013. "Top Incomes and the Measurement of Inequality in Egypt." World Bank Policy Research Working Paper No. 6557, Washington, DC.

Korayem, Karima. 1994. *Poverty and Income Distribution in Egypt*. Third World Forum (Middle East Office), March.

————. 2002. "Pro-Poor Policies in Egypt: Identification and Assessment." *International Journal of Political Economy* 32 (2): 67–96. http://www.jstor.org/stable /40470803.

Radwan, Samir. 1977. *Agrarian Reform and Rural Poverty, Egypt, 1952–1975.* Geneva: International Labor Office.

World Bank. 2007. "Arab Republic of Egypt: Poverty Assessment Update." Vol. 1. Main Report, World Bank, Washington, DC. https://openknowledge.worldbank.org/handle/10986/7642.

————. 2011, *Arab Republic of Egypt: Poverty in Egypt 2008–09: Withstanding the Global Economic Crisis.* Washington, DC: World Bank.

CHAPTER 1

The Measurement of Inequality in the Arab Republic of Egypt: A Historical Survey

Sherine Al-Shawarby

Introduction

Questions of the distribution of income and social justice occupied a prominent position in the Arab Republic of Egypt since the 1930s, although no economic study of the distribution of income on a national scale was published prior to 1952. The earliest comprehensive studies date back to the late 1960s and 1970s (the Central Bank of Egypt 1968; Abdel Fadil 1975; Radwan 1977).

During the last six decades, Egypt has experienced visible swings in inequality, but, if we exclude changes in the distribution of land, these swings have been modest for a country that has experienced all kinds of political and economic changes. War and peace, a transition from a feudal, private sector-led economy before 1952 to a socialist regime in the late 1950s (with redistribution of land and rent control, nationalization of foreign and large-scale domestic private businesses, sequestration of property of the wealthy families, government control of prices and wages, and subsidization of basic foodstuffs), and then to an open economy in 1974 with policies designed to encourage Arab and foreign investment through a series of incentives (trade and balance of payment liberalizations). Such changes in economic policies have also been accompanied by large-scale migration of workers to Arab oil-exporting countries, and repeated economic crises including the external debt crisis in 1982–90, the world food and fuel crisis in 2008, and the global financial crisis from 2008 to the present.

This review covers studies of inequality in Egypt during the last 60 years. The objective is to highlight the change in emphasis and methodologies used for the study of inequality and see whether these studies provide a coherent picture of the evolution of inequality over time. The work is organized as follows: Section 2 traces how inequality has been addressed in the economic literature on Egypt; section 3 reviews the measures and data that have been used in previous studies on inequality in Egypt; section 4 puts together all the findings of previous studies to investigate how inequality evolved in Egypt during the last six decades, and section 5 summarizes the findings.

The Changing Importance of Inequality in the Economic Literature

Egypt was perhaps the first country in the Middle East and North Africa region to manifest concern over social questions. At the conclusion of World War II, the gross disparities of wealth within the Egyptian society started to occupy a major place in the political and social debate among Egyptian politicians and intellectuals (For more details see Abdel-Khalek and Tignor 1982). However, this was not translated into economic studies until the late 1960s.[1] After the 1952 revolution, the implementation of many measures (agrarian reform, progressive taxation, nationalization, confiscation of assets) triggered research appetite, though with some lag, to assess how these changes affected the striking degree of inequality that had characterized income distribution in Egyptian agriculture for a long time. Since then, we can identify four main strands of research that developed almost in chronological order: (i) the distribution of land and the impact of land reforms; (ii) the distributional impact of agricultural and other economic policies; (iii) the urban-rural divide; and (iv) the relation between growth, poverty, and inequality.

Economic studies started with a focus on the *distribution of land in the agriculture sector*, the predominant sector before the revolution.[2] In the mid-1970s, a large body of studies analyzed information about land distribution to trace the developments in the distribution of agricultural landownership and holdings,[3] the main wealth asset in rural areas and in Egypt before the open-door policy in the mid-1970s. Abdel-Fadil (1975) and Radwan (1977), the most cited studies in the literature on inequality in Egypt, made extensive use of large amount of available data to assess the extent to which the changes in land distribution brought by the agrarian reform altered the extreme inequality which characterized the prereform ownership structure in rural Egypt, and affected the income distribution and the social differentiation of the peasantry. Unfortunately, the widespread use of indicators on land distribution in the studies before the 1990s is contrasted by a complete absence of this use afterward.

In the 1980s, the attention given to inequality turned to the **distributional effects of various policies especially on agriculture**. This might be due to the tendency of many prominent Egyptian researchers, mainly socialist, to show the negative distributional impact of the open-door policy that started in 1974 and compare it with the egalitarian impact of socialist policies under Nasser regime. Hence, covering the 1960s and 1970s, Zaytoun (1982) used a larger concept of agricultural income (including income from livestock) to assess income distribution in rural areas. Esfehani (1987)[4] examined the major trends in the agriculture sector of Egypt from 1964 to 1979 to evaluate the factual basis of a number of the then recent agricultural policy debates in Egypt, including income distribution in this sector. Korayem (1981) examined the impact of the implied tax of the pricing policy of the agricultural crops on income distribution, Alderman and von Braun (1984) examined the distributional impact of the Egyptian food subsidy system, and Adams (1989) examined the impact of international remittances on rural income distribution. El-Edel (1982) assessed the impact of direct and indirect taxes on income distribution, Hansen and Radwan (1982) tried to trace the relationship between employment and income distribution, and Levy (1986) examined the changing patterns of income inequality in Egypt in the period 1958–74. More recently, Yitzhaki (1990) and Adams and Ali (1996) assessed the distributional impact of food subsidies. Adams (2002) examined the impact of five sources of income, including nonfarm income, on rural income inequality, while El-Laithy (2008) focused on nonfarm income. Korayem (2008) assessed the impact of trade policy in Egypt (export promotion and import substitution) on income inequality.

Another considerable part of the literature on inequality in Egypt during the 1980s focused on **comparing income distribution between the urban sector and rural sector** and measures the income gap between the two sectors (Korayem 1978, 1981, 1984; El-Samman 1984). Also, Mohie-Eldin (1980) and Korayem (1984) investigated the income disparity among different parts of the urban sector. This work on the urban-rural divide continued in the following decades. Korayem (1994) examined the development of income distribution in rural and urban areas between 1981/82 and 1990/91, and Korayem (2002) provided estimates of income distribution in rural and urban sectors in 1990/91, 1995/96, and 1999/2000 to examine whether policies adopted in Egypt were pro-poor.

More recently, the focus has been on **growth, poverty, and inequality**. Kheir-El-Din and El-Laithy (2006) examined whether growth has been associated with improved distribution during the period 1990/91–2004/05, while Ahmad (2010) investigated if the structure of economic activities at the governorate level explains income disparities and poverty rate differences across Egyptian governorates. Jolliffe, Datt, and Sharma (2004) discussed the technicalities of finding measures of inequality and absolute poverty in Egypt for 1997 which are robust to sample design effects and corrected for spatial variation in price levels. Finally, there are also three reports of the World Bank that measured inequality, though the main focus was on measuring and explaining poverty in Egypt (World Bank 2002, 2007, 2011).

Measures and Data

Although inequality is a multidimensional phenomenon, all studies on Egypt before 2010 measured only one particular dimension of it: income inequality.[5] Since no single measure can be seen as perfect, different measures are usually used to measure inequality of income distribution. The most commonly used of course is the Gini coefficient which is more sensitive to measuring changes in the middle range of a distribution than changes in the tails. Other commonly used measures include (i) macro data using measures such as the relative shares of wages and property income relative to gross domestic product (GDP), (ii) aggregated micro data using measures such as the relative or cumulative shares in total household consumption, and (iii) micro disaggregated data using various measures of inequality. Usually, the choice of a specific measure of inequality depends on the conception of the measure as an index, and more importantly on data availability and the quality of data at hand. In the following, we will trace the measures of inequality and data that have been used in the economic literature of income distribution in Egypt.

For the period before 1952, the portrait of the nature and sources of inequality was drawn from scattered pieces of evidence, with ownership of agriculture land being the most important piece of information. In the 1960s and 1970s, a period where the focus was on inequality in the distribution of agricultural land holdings and landownership, most of the studies calculated Gini coefficients for the distribution of landholdings or landownership using data from the 1961 agricultural census (Central Bank of Egypt 1968; Radwan 1977), CAPMAS agricultural holdings, the Ministry of Agriculture data—mostly unpublished (Zaytoun 1982), or surveys conducted for specific research purposes (Zaytoun 1982;[6] Hansen and Radwan 1982[7]).

Since the late 1960s, Family Budget Surveys (FBS), also known as Household Income, Expenditure and Consumption Surveys (HIECS) since 1990/91, have become one of the most important sources of information on Egypt's income distribution. Between 1959 and 2009, nine surveys were conducted. There are various differences between these surveys, making the intertemporal comparability of their estimates statistically inaccurate (see box 1.1). With these new data, the Gini was commonly used to measure inequality in consumption expenditure distribution, mostly using grouped data from the HIECS as disaggregated individual files were not made available to researchers (Abdel-Fadil 1975; Radwan 1977; El-Edel 1982;

Box 1.1 Household Consumption Expenditure Data: Historical Review of Differences

The differences across time between Family Budget Surveys (FBS) in terms of definitions, concepts, questionnaire design, sampling design, size and procedures, and so on… raise statistical difficulties concerning the accuracy and comaparability of different estimates of income distribution that are reviewed in this paper. Therefore, intertemporal comparisons of scattered findings based on sample surveys' data, and the procedure of inferring a trend should be interpreted cautiously.

Very little is known about the methodological characteristics of the FBS in the years before 1981/82. All what is found are a few lines in the manuals of later surveys describing few aspects that are reported hereunder.

The first survey of income and expenditure, planned to be a pilot, was undertaken in 1955 by the committee of statistic in three villages of Giza governorate (4,000 households) on a

box continues next page

**Box 1.1 Household Consumption Expenditure Data: Historical Review
of Differences** (continued)

sample of 750 households. In 1958/59, the committee conducted the first national survey in all governorates of Egypt with a sample of 6,376 households distributed between urban and rural with a percentage of 51.5 and 48.5 percent, respectively. All sample households were observed for the entire survey period. Starting from the second survey, the Central Agency of Public Mobilization and Statistics (CAPMAS) has taken over the responsibility of collecting household data. The second and third surveys were held in 1964/65 and 1974/75 on a larger sample (of 13,818 and 11,995 households, respectively) and a larger share of urban areas (67.6 percent). The sample was divided into four subsamples where households of each sub-sample were observed for only three consecutive months.[a]

In 1981/82, the fourth survey was conducted on a sample of 17,000 households distributed equally between urban and rural areas. A new survey methodology combining fixed and changeable surveyed households was applied. A subsample of 1,000 households was observed throughout the entire survey period (12 months) while the remaining 16,000 households were divided into four subsamples and observed for only three consecutive months. Also, the questionnaire of 1981/82 survey included various new tables on consumption expenditure and classification of households and individuals in the sample, and new goods and services.

In 1990/91, many changes were introduced, starting with the name of the survey that changed from "Household Budget Survey" to "Income, Expenditure and Consumption Survey," or HIECS. The fifth survey had a sample of 15,000 households, with 60 percent of them in urban areas and 40 percent in rural areas. The entire sample was divided into 12 subsamples, each being observed for only one month. Also, instead of only two visits (one in the beginning of the round and one in the end) to households by interviewers, the number increased to 10 to ensure more accurate reporting of data. The supplementary form has become an essential source of information on consumption and expenditure data.

In 1995/96, the sixth survey was conducted with 15,090 households, of which 45.1 percent in urban areas and 54.9 percent in rural areas. The same survey scheme of the 1990/91 survey was applied, that is, households were observed for one month only. The number of goods and services in the questionnaire increased from 490 in 1990/91 to 550 in 1995/96. In 1999/2000, the sample of the seventh survey increased to include 48,000 households, of which 60 percent in urban areas and 40 percent in rural areas. The entire sample was divided into 12 subsamples, each being observed for only one month. In 2004/05, the distribution of the sample between urban areas and rural areas changed (53.6 and 46.4 percent, respectively), and for the first time the classification of individual consumption according to purpose (COICOP) in designing the expenditure and consumption questionnaire was used, and expenditure on used commodities (durables and semi durables) as well as data related to change in assets owned by the household during the reference year were added. In 2008/09, the sample size remained the same but it was divided into 24 subsamples, each being observed for 15 days. Also, the number of primary sampling units (PSUs) from which the sample was withdrawn increased from 12,000 as in 2004/05 survey to 2,526, with 20 households being selected in each PSU instead of 40. Also, some questions on contributions and benefits from social security and contributions to health insurance were added.

El-Issawy 1982; Korayem 1984; Adams 1985; Levy 1986; Adams and Ali 1996; Ahmad 2010). It was only in the early 2000s that a restricted access to the detailed disaggregated data has been possible (Kheir-El-Din and El-Laithy 2006; World Bank 2002, 2007, 2011). To overcome data accessibility, some studies estimated the Gini coefficient mostly using household data that were collected specifically for a certain project and of much smaller sample size than the HIECS (Zaytoun 1982; Hansen and Radwan 1982; Radwan and Lee 1986; Yitzhaki 1990; Adams 1991).

There are also some other indicators of inequality in consumption expenditure that are calculated from HIECS and are very often associated with the measurement of the Gini coefficient. The most commonly used is the calculation of relative shares in total household consumption expenditure by quantile group. Radwan (1977), El-Issawy (1982), Hansen and Radwan (1982), Hansen (1991), Korayem (1994, 2002), and World Bank (1991, 2007) provided estimates of these shares. The cumulative percentage share of consumption expenditure bracket, the basic information to draw the Lorenz curve, is also commonly used (El-Kholi 1973; Abdel-Fadil 1975; Radwan 1977). Also, aggregated FBS and HIECS data were used to measure the gap between rural and urban areas (Korayem 1978; El-Issawy 1979; Korayem 1981, 1984).

Some other studies used the national accounts data produced by the Ministry of Planning to examine the behavior of **factor shares**, wages and property returns, in national income. The higher this ratio, the higher will be the share of GDP allocated to the wage earners who belong to the lowest income group of people (Hansen 1968; Abdel-Fadil 1975; Radwan 1977; Mohie-ElDin 1980; El-Issawy 1982; Hansen and Radwan 1982; Esfehani 1987; Korayem 2008). Finally, it is worth mentioning the other indicators that were used, though much less frequently, in the surveyed studies. For example, the coefficient of variation and standard variation of logs of consumption expenditure distribution (Abdel-Fadil 1975); TDM or total disparities measures suggested by Kuznets (Levy 1986); the Theil coefficient (Adams 1989; World Bank 1991), and the Income Inequality Index (III) constructed by Korayem (2002).[8]

Evolution of Inequality

In spite of the above-mentioned lack of economic studies on inequality in Egypt prior to 1952, there was unanimity among commentators that Egypt's wealth was grossly maldistributed in this period. According to Radwan (1977), the Gini coefficient for the distribution of landownership increased from 0.696 in 1896 to 0.758 in 1952. So, on the eve of the First Agrarian Reform of 1952, large landlords, owning over 50 feddans,[9] numbered less than 0.5 percent of the total number of proprietors. It is not surprising, therefore, that Egypt was then described as the "half percent society" (Eshag and Kamal 1968).

In terms of functional income distribution in agriculture, the then predominant sector in Egypt, some estimates point to a shift in the distribution of agricultural factor income from rent of land and possibly capital to wages. The size of this shift is different from one source to the other. Hansen (1991) reports an increase in the labor's share of agricultural income from about one third in 1900 to almost one-half in 1938, at the expense of a decline in the share of land rent from almost one-half to almost 40 percent; with no further change until the land reforms of 1952. Estimates of labor's share in Hansen (1968) were found roughly unchanged (at 35 percent of the total agriculture output value) between 1900 and 1951. In both cases, the author acknowledged that these are uncertain estimates, especially for labor's share.

In what follows, we will trace the evolution of inequality in Egypt as revealed by the findings of previous work that addressed income and assets distribution. The period that we cover starts from the early 1950s when solid information on the size of inequality in Egypt started to be available. In order to portray a coherent story about inequality developments in Egypt, our survey will focus on studies that used comparable measures, allowing inferring a trend. This section will thus present the findings related to the distribution of land, and to distribution of income based on the consumption expenditure. The gap between rural and urban sectors is not the scope of this study, since intertemporal comparison using the results of various studies is not very straightforward, because it is not always clear if per capita income data are in nominal or real terms, which deflator is used and if the base year of this deflator is the same across different studies. Also, because consumption expenditure brackets are not always the same across different time, and because with time the higher consumption expenditure brackets would tend to include higher shares of the population, we decided to exclude the distribution of cumulative percentage share of consumption expenditure bracket across different studies from our coverage. Finally, estimates of inequality for one given year are excluded, since they will not help in tracing the evolution of inequality in Egypt.

Inequality in Land Distribution

According to the various studies that attempted to examine the distributional impact of the agrarian reform on rural incomes, there is evidence that the disappearance of the very large estates following the first agrarian reform of 1952 reduced the flagrant degree of inequality. As shown in table 1.1, estimates of the Gini coefficient of the distribution of land holdings and landownerships indicate a downward trend between 1950 and 1979. Radwan (1977), one of the key studies on the distributional impact of the agrarian reform in Egypt, found a slight decline in the Gini coefficient of the distribution of landholdings between 1950 and 1961 (from 0.889 to 0.800), indicating a moderate movement toward less inequality. The equalizing trend was more significant in the years after as demonstrated by Zaytoun (1982). Her estimates of the Gini coefficient show a decline from 0.64 in 1961 to 0.53 in 1965 and to 0.46 in 1974/75, before picking up again in the following years. The trend in the distribution of landownership followed a similar course, although the gap between estimates is very large. While Central Bank (1968) shows that the Gini coefficient of the distribution of landownership fell from 0.611 before the 1952 reform to 0.432 in 1961 and to 0.383 in 1965, Hansen 1991 shows a decline from 0.74 in 1950 to 0.66 in 1977/78.

Table 1.1 Gini Coeffcient of Land Holdings and Ownerships, 1950–79

	Holdings						Ownerships			
	1950	1961	1965	1974/75	1977–78	1979	1950	1961	1965	1977–78
Central Bank 1968							0.61	0.432	0.383	
Samir Radwan 1977	0.889	0.8						0.43	0.38	
Zaytoun 1982		0.64	0.53	0.46	0.48	0.55				
Hansen 1991	0.68				0.48		0.74			0.66

Sources: Central bank of Egypt 1968; Radwan 1977; Zaytoun 1982; Hansen 1991.

Also, the results of the analysis of the distribution of land by decile reveals that in spite of the important phase of agrarian reform, land remained flagrantly unequally distributed in Egypt. The columns of Radwan (1977) in table 1.2 show that in 1961 the bottom 40 percent of the rural population had no land and half the population controlled only 1 percent; the top 10 percent controlled about 65 percent of the land. Radwan also stated that the effect of the 1952 land reform[10] was limited to the two extremes of landownership: the large and the small without affecting in any way the landless peasants since land distribution was limited to previous tenants and small farmers. Zaytoun (1982) extended the analysis to the 1970s and her findings corroborated Radwan's findings. More specifically, she found that the first two agrarian reforms (in 1952 and 1961) significantly affected the small landowners, whose share of cultivated land increased from 35.4 percent before 1952 to 57.1 percent in 1965, and big landowners, whose share drastically declined from 34 percent to 12.6 percent over the same period. She found also that 82 percent of the landholders held 45 percent of the land in 19977/78 and that 2.4 percent of the landholders, holding 10 or more feddans, held 22.3 percent of the land. Her findings corroborate the conclusion that the middle peasants (those owing over 10 feddans) had become the real power in the countryside and are successors to the dispossessed elite.

Hansen and Radwan (1982) analyzed a 1977 ILO survey and found that the reduction in inequality effect of the three reform laws was reversed by 1977, and that since the mid-1960s inequalities increased. The share of small owners (<5 feddans) fell from 57 to 52 percent between 1965 and 1977, with the gain going to the group of medium-sized landowners, whose share increased from 30 to around 34 percent. With the same ILO data Hansen (1991) found that between 1950 and 1977/78 there was only a slight equalization of landownership and holdings. The share of the first quintile increased in both cases, with the largest increase being in the share of medium-sized ownership (see table 1.2). Information from the 1982 agricultural census indicates a certain strong reversal of the tendency of land holding distribution to become more equal.

In view of the foregoing review, it is safe to conclude that the period 1950–77 had a U-shaped pattern of agricultural land distribution, as the equalizing pattern witnessed in 1961 and 1965 was reversed afterward. Also, a substantial gap remained between the very small holders and the large holders regarding each group's share in total area cultivated, and the trend of consolidation of the group of medium-sized landowners continued.

Table 1.2 Decile Distribution of Landholdings in Egypt, 1950 and 1961

	Holdings				Ownership	
	1950	1950	1961	1977/78	1950	1977/78
	Radwan 1977	Hansen 1991	Radwan 1977	Hansen 1991	Hansen 1991	
1st decile	0		0			
2nd decile	0		0			
1st quintile	0	2	0	6	4	5
3rd decile	0		0			
4th decile	0		0			
5th decile	0		1			
6th decile	0		2.54			
7th decile	2.31		6.21			
8th decile	16.05		9.62			
2nd to 4th quintile	18.36	25	19.37	41	18	25
9th decile	12.03		15.67			
10th decile	79.61		64.96			
Top quintile	91.64	73	80.63	53	78	70
Gini	0.889	0.68	0.8	0.48	0.74	0.66
Mean size (hectares)		2.6		0.8	0.9	0.7
Mena size, feddans (World Bank 1991)		3.8		2	5.2	1.6

Source: Radwan 1977; Hansen 1991.

Inequality in Income and Expenditure

Knowledge about income distribution is usually based on inference from expenditure and income surveys. Egypt's household surveys are not all strictly comparable, given changes introduced to sample and questionnaire design. Therefore, it is not quite correct to establish a long-term trend of income distribution based on the results scattered in previous studies. However, it is worth summarizing the different measures that have been published to date.

Summary Measures

As previously mentioned, the most commonly used summary measure for inequality has been the Gini coefficient. As shown in table 1.3, which provides Gini coefficients for private household consumption expenditure, the Gini declined persistently between 1958/59 and 1974/75 (from 0.42 to 0.38) at the national level (Radwan 1977), and fluctuated afterward.[11] There are no estimates of the Gini for the period between 1974/75, 1981/82, and 1990/91. However, a deterioration of income distribution at the national level can be inferred from the estimates of the income Gini in rural and urban areas provided by Korayem (1994) for 1981/82 and 1990/91. Kheir-El-Din and El-Laithy (2006) showed a decline in Gini (from 0.45 to 0.35) between 1990/91 and 1995/96, an increase in 1999/2000 (to 0.36), and then a decline in 2004/05 (0.32). World Bank (2007) had the same Gini estimates as those in Kheir-El-Din and EL-Laithy (2006) for the years 1995/96, 1999/2000, and 2004/05. Finally, World Bank

Table 1.3 Selected Summary Measures, 1958/59–2008/09

Year	Rural areas								Urban							Egypt				
						World Bank 2007						World Bank 2007								
	Adams	Radwan 1977	El-Issay 1982	Korayem 1994	Korayem 2002	Lower Egypt	Upper Egypt	World Bank 2011	El-Issawy 1982	Korayem 1994	Korayem 2002	Metropol-itans	Lower Egypt	Upper Egypt	World Bank 2011	El-Issawy 1982	Kheir-El-Din and El-Laithy 2006	World Bank 2007	World Bank 2011	Ahmad 2010
1958/59	0.34	0.373	0.37						0.40							0.42				
1964/65	0.29	0.353	0.35						0.40							0.40				
1974/75	0.35	0.392	0.35						0.37							0.38				
1977*																				
1982	0.34			0.29						0.32										
1990/91				0.32	0.283					0.38	0.304						0.446			
1995/96					0.275	0.209	0.241				0.326	0.36	0.27	0.35			0.345	0.345		0.345
1999/2000					0.255	0.211	0.24				0.35	0.37	0.257	0.368			0.362	0.361		
2004/05						0.228	0.247	0.22				0.34	0.282	0.372	0.34		0.32	0.32	0.313	
2008/09								0.216							0.333				0.307	

Source: World Bank data.

Based on the data generated from a survey carried out by the International Labour Organization (ILO) in 1977.

(2011) showed a continued improvement of income distribution between 2004/05 and 2008/09 (down from 0.31 to 0.307).

Taken at face value, the comparison of all these results indicate that (i) in general, since 1958/59 the Egyptian income distribution has been relatively egalitarian by the standards of developing countries (with a peak of 0.446 in 1990/91 and a dip of 0.307 in 2008/09); (ii) the narrow range of fluctuation points to the relative stability of income inequality in Egypt in spite of the many drastic changes and shocks the economy has faced over this long period of time; (iii) there is a marked discrepancy in the estimates of Gini for private household consumption for a given year between surveyed studies, and sometimes even between studies of the same author (estimates of Korayem and World Bank); and (iv) income distribution improved between 1991/92 and 2008/09 from 0.45 to around 0.31. Overall, we can trace the development of income distribution between subperiods in the last 50 years, but we cannot strictly use the value of these estimates across time comparison to affirm whether inequality improved between 1958/59 and 2008/09.

With respect to the distribution of private household expenditure in rural and urban areas, estimates of various studies provide a consistent story about income inequality evolvement between 1958/59 and 2004/05. There is evidence that in rural areas the income distribution deteriorated (or at least did not improve) in the years 1974/75, 1990/91, 1999/2000, and 2004/05.[12] In urban areas, inequality worsened or remained almost unchanged throughout the period, except for a slight improvement taking place between 1964/65 and 1974/75 (see table 1.3).[13] Other summary measures, like the Theil entropy measure and the Income Inequality Index (III), followed the same path as the Gini coefficient in the years for which they are available. Finally, rural areas have been characterized by a slightly more equitable distribution than urban areas, as reflected by the low value of the Gini coefficient and the III measure in rural areas. Of course, this does not imply that rural households are better off than urban ones in terms of expenditures (income).

It is worth mentioning that in the 1970s and 1980s, there were complaints that Egyptian data were not abundant, many basic sources were lacking and what was available had many shortcomings, and that data of income distribution were not published (Abdel-Khalek and Tignor 1982). Also, it has been always argued that the household data used to measure inequality are likely to make income distribution seem more equitable than it really is, and that values of the Gini coefficient based on the Egyptian data do not reveal as bleak a picture as is generally found in developing economies. Explanations provided in these studies were various: (i) Household surveys usually tend to not capture the tails of the distribution: it is very difficult to obtain information on the very poor who do not have stable dwellings places, and at the other end of the distribution, the rich often do not report their income fully; (ii) if the pattern of savings is properly taken into account, much higher Gini coefficients would emerge for the distribution of income than is suggested by the distribution of household consumption; (iii) the

Gini coefficient itself is so highly aggregated as to be misleading in many ways; and, finally, (iv) in a country in which the economy and society are so thoroughly penetrated by the state, the Gini coefficient cannot measure the impact of many public goods and services on household income (Abdel-Khalek and Tignor 1982). We can add to this that the use of aggregated data would yield lower Gini coefficients. As with other inequality coefficients, the Gini coefficient is influenced by the granularity of the measurements. For example, quintiles (low granularity) will usually yield a lower Gini coefficient than ventiles (high granularity) if taken from the same distribution.

Distributions by Quantiles

To set a comparison between the results of the distribution of annual consumption expenditure in the surveyed studies, we calculated the shares of common aggregate groups from the available shares of expenditures in these studies. (See the bold underlined numbers in italics in table 1.4). Here again, marked discrep-

Table 1.4 Distribution of Annual Consumption Expenditure

	Rural															
	El-Issawy			*Radwan 1977 and Hansen and Radwan 1982*				*World Bank1991*				*Korayem 1994, 2002*		*Korayem 2008*		
	1958/ 59	*1964/ 65*	*1974/ 75*	*1958/ 59*	*1964/ 65*	*1974/ 75*	*1977*	*1958/ 59*	*1964/ 65*	*1974/ 75*	*1981/ 82*	*1981/ 82*	*1991/ 92*	*1990/ 91*	*1995/ 96*	*1999/ 2000*
Lowest decile												2.7	2.8	3.4	3.2	3.7
2nd decile												4.9	4.8	5.2	5.2	5.6
Lowest quintile				6.35	6.95	5.8	5.4	6.7	7.4	5.9	6	*7.6*	*7.6*	**8.6**	**8.4**	*9.3*
												6	*6*	*6*	*5.8605*	*6.48837*
3rd decile												6.3	5.9	6	6.3	6.7
4th decile												7.4	6.6	7.6	7.7	7.5
Second quintile				11.29	11.85	11.27	10.9	11	11.6	11.2	11.4	*13.7*	*12.5*	*13.6*	*14*	14.2
Lowest 40%	17.65	19.0	18.84	*17.64*	*18.8*	***17.07***	*16.3*	*17.7*	*19.0*	***17.1***	*17.4*	***21.3***	*20.1*	***22.2***	*22.4*	*23.5*
5th decile												8.4	7.8	8.1	8.6	8.6
6th decile												9.5	9	9.3	9.5	9.6
Third quintile				15.65	16.07	15.71	15.7	**16.6**	**16.3**	15.8	16	***17.9***	*16.8*	***17.4***	*18.1*	*18.2*
Lowest 60%	34.24	35.26	35.46	***33.29***	***34.87***	***32.78***	*32*	*34.3*	*35.3*	***32.9***	*33.4*	***39.2***	*36.9*	***39.6***	*40.5*	*41.7*
7th decile												10.8	10.1	10.6	10.8	11
Middle 30% (5th+6th+7th decile)	37.74	37.28	37.8									*28.7*	*26.9*	**28**	*28.9*	*29.2*
8th decile												12.2	12	12.3	12.1	11.8
4th quintile				22.78	22.41	21.09	22.8	21.9	22	21.2	22.6	*23.0*	*22.1*	***22.9***	*22.9*	*22.8*
9th decile												14.7	14.6	14.4	14.4	14.3
Top decile	28.02	27.46	26.74	28.22	27.52	**31.01**	29					23	26.5	**23.2**	22.1	21.4
Top quintile				43.93	42.72	46.13	45.2	43.9	42.7	**45.9**	44	***37.7***	*41.1*	***37.6***	*36.5*	*35.7*
Gini coefficient	0.37	0.35	0.35	0.37	0.35	**0.392**	0.39	**0.36**	**0.29**	0.35	0.34	0.29	0.32	**0.283**	0.275	0.255
Theil measures								0.16	0.12	0.17	0.17			0.227	0.216	0.204

Source: World Bank data.

ancies between estimates for a given year are observed (see the shaded numbers in table 1.4). We can trace the direction of the path of income distribution as long as estimates of shares of income distribution overlap in time. Accordingly, we could set a trend for the rural and urban sectors areas between 1958/59 and 1999/2000, but not at the national level because of the gap in estimates between 1974/75 and 1995/96.

Estimates of rural income shares in El-Issawy (1982), Radwan (1977), and World Bank (1991) indicate that from 1958/59 to 1964/65 there was a small gain in the share of consumption expenditure of the bottom 40 percent, against a slight drop in the share of the top 10 percent. Between 1964/65 and 1974/75, the main gainers and losers from the changes in income distribution are not clear. While El-Issawy (1982) found that the middle 30 percent gained at the expense of the top decile, Radwan (1977) and World Bank (1991) found that the top 20 percent gained an increased share of consumption expenditure at the expense of the lowest 40 percent. Between 1974/75 and 1981/82, it was mainly the share

Urban										Overall Egypt					
El-Issawy			World Bank 1991		Korayem 1994, 2002		Korayem 2000, 2008			El-Issawy 1982			World Bank 2007		
1958/59	1964/65	1974/75	1974/75	1981/82	1981/82	1991/92	1990/91	1995/96	1999/2000	1958/59	1964/65	1974/75	1995/96	1999/2000	2004/05
					2.6	2.5	3.3	2.9	3				4.2	3.9	3.8
					1.8	4.3	5	4.6	4.4				5.4	5.1	5.1
			8.1	7.5	4.4	6.8	8.3	7.5	7.4				9.6	9.0	8.9
					6	4.9	6.2	5.7	5.5				6.2	5.9	6
					6.9	6.2	6.9	6.7	6.4				6.9	6.6	6.7
			12.7	13.2	12.9	11.1	13.1	12.4	11.9				13.1	12.5	12.7
16.41	16.49	18.31	20.8	20.7	17.3	17.9	21.4	19.9	19.3	16.25	17.05	17.62	22.7	21.5	21.6
					8	6.7	7.7	7.9	7.5				7.7	7.4	7.6
					9	8.5	9	8.8	8.2				8.6	8.3	8.5
			16.7	17.2	17.0	15.2	16.7	16.7	15.7				16.3	15.7	16.1
30.89	31.25	34.39	37.5	37.9	34.3	33.1	38.1	36.6	35	30.56	31.63	33.62	39	37.2	37.7
					10.3	9	10.3	10.3	9.5				9.8	9.5	9.6
38.73	37.99	38.01			27.3	24.2	27.0	27.0	25.2	37.31	32.24	37.86	26.1	25.2	25.7
					11.9	11.2	11.8	11.7	11.4				11.3	11.1	11.2
			22.8	22.3	22.2	20.2	22.1	22	20.9				21.1	20.6	20.8
					14.6	14.2	14.7	14.9	14.9				14.1	13.9	14
30.38	30.76	27.6			25.9	32.6	25.2	26.4	29.4	32.13	31.13	28.52	26	28.3	27.6
			39.7	39.8	40.5	46.8	39.9	41.3	44.3				40.1	42.2	41.6
0.4	0.4	0.37	0.37	0.37	0.32	0.38	0.304	0.326	0.35	0.42	0.4	0.38	0.345	0.361	0.321
							0.244	0.259	0.285						

of consumption expenditure of the 4th quintile that had the largest increase at the expense of that of the top 20 percent (World Bank 1991). Between 1981/82 and 1990/91, the significant gains of the top 10 percent were at the expense of all other groups (Korayem 1994). Between 1990/91 and 1994/95, the slight gain of the lowest 40 percent and significant gain of the middle 30 percent class were at the expense of the loss of the top 20 percent. Finally, between 1994/95 and 1999/2000, the gain in the share of consumption expenditure of the lowest 40 percent was against the loss of the top 10 percent.

In urban areas, the degree of inequality in household consumption remained virtually unchanged between 1958/59 and the mid-1960s, and then showed some improvement over the following decade (El-Issawy 1981). Income distribution has remained almost unchanged between 1974/75 and 1981/82 (World Bank 1991), before deteriorating in favor of the top decile throughout the following decades, with the poorest 20 percent sharing some of the redistribution gains only in 1990/91.

Whether inequality of income distribution increased between 1958/59 and 1999/2000, it is hard to tell from the available estimates of distribution of income shares. The changes are too small to justify any firm conclusion about the trend in income distribution, all we can say perhaps is that the flagrant inequalities which characterized the rural income inequality in the 1950s improved in the mid-1960s but most probably it has fluctuated around the same pattern in the following four decades. Also, although losses in the income shares of the poorest groups were larger in the urban sector than in the rural sector, and consequently the gains of the richest groups were larger in the urban sector than in the rural sector, it is not clear if the income distribution has significantly changed over the 50 years considered.

Income Shares of Factors of Production

One way of presenting the overall changes in the matrix of income distribution is to look at the changes in income shares accruing to labor. Table 1.5 summarizes the available information of the relative shares of wages in the Egyptian economy.[14] Three types of labor income shares were calculated in the surveyed studies. The first is the share of agricultural wages to agricultural GDP (Abdel-Fadil 1975; Radwan 1977; El-Issawy 1982; Mohie-Eldin 1980), the second is the share of wages in the industrial sector or nonagricultural sector to GDP, and the last is the share of nationwide wages to GDP. The last available estimates of these shares go back to mid-1970s for the share of agricultural wages and of industrial sector wages, to early 1982 for nonagricultural wages, and to early 1990s for the nationwide wages to GDP.

Agricultural sector. It is clear from table 1.5 that there was a marked increase in the share of agricultural wages to agricultural GDP from 17 to 33 percent between 1951/52 and 1966/67 (Abdel-Fadil 1975). Between 1967/68 and 1974, a movement in the opposite direction is observed, with the share of wages falling to 22 percent by 1974 (Abdel-Fadil 1975; Radwan 1977). However, Abdel-Fadil put serious reservations on this increase, since he found that money-wage rates remained almost constant throughout the 1960s, and it is very doubtful that the increase in the absolute size of the share of wages over this period reflects an increase in the employment opportunities for agricultural wage laborers. El-Issawy (1982), which covered the period between 1950 and 1975/76, used the figures of Abdel-Fadil, and extended the analysis until 1975/76. He found that the share of wages in 1976 (25.7 percent) was only 1.5 percentage points above its 1959/60 level. This means that most of the improvement in the distribution of agricultural income by factors shares achieved between 1952 and mid-1960s has been eroded between 1967 and 1974. Mohie-Eldin (1982) findings are consistent in trend with this inverse U-shape of the share of rural wages in value added in agriculture between 1959 and 1974. He also found that in 1975, the share rose again and stabilized at 28 percent in 1976.

However, most of these studies highlighted that these figures should be treated with caution. Abdel-Fadil (1975) and Radwan (1977) argued that official data tend to overestimate agricultural wages, because they represent "imputed" average annual wages for the entire agricultural labor force (including unpaid family labor and landholders working on their own account), rather than wages paid in cash or kind. El-Issawy (1979) explained that this implies three types of errors in the wages series: (i) errors in estimating annual average wage rates by farm operating, (ii) errors in calculating imputed wages, and (iii) errors in estimating agricultural employment which arise from inaccurate estimation of both labor requirements by crop and actual number of working days per day. However, he concluded that since the concern is with the trends over time rather than with precise magnitude at specific points in time, this bias is not important. Accordingly, it is safe to say that the available figures give a fairly reasonable, though tentative, picture of the changes occurred in the functional distribution of agricultural income over the period 1952–76. Esfehani (1987) also examines the trends in the factor distribution of income in agriculture in order to understand how it responded to the changes in the sector, in the context of studying the aggregate behavior of crop production in Egypt. He estimated the shares of labor wage in total crop revenue in Egypt between 1964 and 1979, and found the same trends in the evolution of income distribution. However, Esfehani's estimates of labor shares in agricultural income seem to be rather high when compared with the estimates of Mohie-Eldin (1982, see table 1.5).

Nonagricultural sector. Few studies traced the movements over time of the share of wages in industrial and nonagricultural income. Table 1.5 shows the estimates of the two studies we found: El-Issawy (1982) which covers the period 1952–1975/76 and Hansen (1991) that extends the analysis to 1981/82. For reasons similar to those mentioned with respect to errors of measuring agricultural wages, there are many shortcomings in the estimates of the table. Information about employment and wage rate is incomplete; wage income is difficult to define and compute for certain categories of labor; remittances may include nonwage income.

However, the two studies point to an increase in the share of wages in both the industrial and nonagricultural sectors between 1952 and 1959/60, a reversal

Table 1.5 Summary of Studies on Wages

	Wages % of agricultural GDP				Wages of industrial sector % of GDP	Wages of nonagricultural sector						National wages % of GDP		
						% nonagricultural income		% GDP		% total domestic private income	% total private income, incl, remittances			
	Abdel-Fadil 1975	Radwan 1977	El-Issawy 1982	Moheod-din 1982	El-Issawy 1982	El-Issawy 1982	Hansen 1991	Hansen and Radwan 1982	Hansen 1991	Hansen and Radwan 1982	Hansen and Radwan 1982	El-Issawy 1982	Korayem 2008	Hansen and Radwan 1982
14														
1951/52	17	17	17		41.8							38		
1959/60	24	24	24.2	24.2	48.1	53.7	53.7					44.8		
1960/61	25	25		24.5										
1961/62	31	31		31.3										
1962/63	30	30		29.7										
1963/64	29	29		29.3										
1964/65	32	32		31.7										
1960/61–64/65	**29.4**	**29.4**	27.8	29.3	45.7	53.2	53.2					46.1		
19665/66	32	32		32.9										
1966/67	33	33		32.9										
1965/66–66/67	**32.5**	**32.5**	32.93	31.22	45.7	54.6	54.6					49.2		
1967/68	31	31		31.9										
1968/69	31	31		30.6										
1967/68–69/70	**31**	**31**	30	31.904	47	57.6	57.6							
1969/70	28	28		28.2										
1970/71		29		28.8										
1971/72		27		26.5										
1972		25												
1973		24		23.1										
1974		22		23.2	48.3	60.3	60.3	42.4	42.4	52.9	54.3	49.6	49.5	

table continues next page

Table 1.5 Summary of Studies on Wages *(continued)*

	Wages % of agricultural GDP				Wages of industrial sector % of GDP	Wages of nonagricultural sector								
	Abdel-Fadil	Radwan	El-Issawy	Moheod-din	El-Issawy	% nonagricultural income		% GDP		% total domestic private income	% total private income, incl, remittances	National wages % of GDP		
						El-Issawy	Hansen	Hansen and Radwan	Hansen	Hansen and Radwan	Hansen and Radwan	El-Issawy	Korayem	Hansen and Radwan
	1975	1977	1982	1982	1982	1982	1991	1982	1991	1982	1982	1982	2008	1982
1970/71–1974	25.3	**25.4**	25.3	25.4										42.4
1975				28.3				43.2	43.2	55.1	57.5			43.2
1975/1976			25.3	28.3	43.3	52.2	52.2					44.1		
1976							45	44.7	44.7	57.4	61.3	42.5		44.7
1977								44.1	44.1	57.1	61.3			44.1
1978								43	43	56.5	63.1			43
1979							36.9	42.9	42.9	58.5	64.8			42.9
1981/82							42.1		46.3					
1984/85													39.2	
1986/87									37.6					
1990/91													28.9	

Source: El-Issawy 1979, 1981; Abdel-Khalek 1981; Korayem 2008.

Note: Wages refer to paid and imputed wages and are subject to three types of errors (see El-Issawy 1981, 90). Property is calculated as residuals. GDP = gross domestic product.

in this trend in the period 1960/61–1964/65 and a stagnation in 1965/67–1966/67. A pickup is observed until 1974, before a significant fall in 1975/76, when wages accounted for a smaller percentage of income in both sectors than in 1959/60 (43.3 percent against 48.1 percent in industry and 52.2 percent against 53.7 percent in the nonagricultural sector). The downward trend in the share of wages in nonagricultural income continued until 1979 and reversed in 1981/82 to reach 42.1 percent.

Hansen also found that from 1974 to 1979 the share of wages in nonagriculture sector to GDP was almost constant while its share in domestically generated private income (excluding income from Suez Canal and the petroleum sector) increased steadily. The difference is attributed to the rapid increase in canal tolls and petroleum revenue, which accrue to the government sector. When workers' remittances are included in private income, the wage share increases strongly from 54 percent in 1974 to 65 percent in 1979. During the 1980s, the share in total GDP appears to have decreased consistently. If these data are to be used as a proxy for factorial income distribution, the conclusion would be that the years 1970/71–76 witnessed deterioration in urban income distribution. This conclusion was qualified as "not implausible," given the large profits that are being made in the urban real estate market alone (Hansen 1991).

National level. As shown in table 1.5, the first half of the 1960s witnessed a steady increase in the share of wages, due probably to impressive rates of increase of employment and real wages during this period (El-Issawy 1982). This period was one of major structural change, with the industrial sector growing much faster than the agricultural sector. In the period 1965/66–74, the share of wages was fairly stable around the 49 percent mark. This was largely due to the slowing down of the rates of increase of employment and wage rates and the sluggish growth of GDP itself during this period. Starting from the mid-1970s, the share of wages began to decline falling persistently from 50 percent in 1970/71 to 28.9 percent in 1990/91 (Korayem 2008).

Conclusion

Studies on inequality in Egypt have roughly followed three distinct periods. Early studies focused on land inequalities and the rural sector and were conducted in the background of major land reforms in the 1950s and 1960s. The following period was characterized by studies of inequality across urban and rural areas in line with the period of strong emigration and urbanization flows that characterized the 1970s and 1980s. The 1990s and the most recent decade have seen perhaps a decline in the interest for inequality as growth, liberalization, and privatization of the economy attracted most of the attention and the studies of inequalities that appeared did so mostly in the context of poverty studies.

Different measures were used to measure inequality in the surveyed studies, but the Gini coefficient has been the most commonly used. One of the most important sources of information on Egypt's income distribution since the late 1960s have been the Family Budget Surveys (FBS), known as Household Income,

Expenditure and Consumption Surveys (HIECS) since 1990/91. Between 1959 and 2009, nine surveys were conducted with various differences between them, making the intertemporal comparability of their estimates statistically inaccurate. In addition, it was only in the 2000s that a few researchers started to have access to the full household dataset. Before 2000, only aggregated FBS and HIECS data were used to measure inequality in Egypt.

The review of studies on inequality since the 1950s has pinpointed the following facts: (i) Since 1958/59, the Egyptian income distribution has been relatively egalitarian by the standards of developing countries with a peak of 0.45 in 1990/91 and a dip of 0.31 in 2008/09; (ii) the range in which inequality has fluctuated over the 60 years considered is relatively narrow considering the many drastic changes and shocks that the economy has faced over this long period of time; (iii) there is a marked discrepancy in the estimates of the Gini for household consumption for any given year between different studies, and sometimes even between studies of the same authors.

Overall, it is possible to trace the development of income distribution between subperiods in the last 50 years, but we cannot strictly use the values of these estimates to affirm whether inequality improved or not between 1958/59 and 2008/09. The changes are too small to justify any firm conclusion about the trend in income distribution. All we can say is that the flagrant inequalities which characterized rural areas in the 1950s improved in the mid-1960s but most probably fluctuated around the same values during the following decades. Although losses in the income shares of the poorest groups were larger in the urban sector than in the rural sector, and consequently the gains of the richest groups were larger in the urban sector than in the rural sector, it is not clear if the income distribution has significantly changed over the last 50 years.

Notes

1. There were studies on the agriculture sector and its revenue that contain useful information for understanding the equity status in Egypt before 1952 (for example, Willcocks 1899; Willcocks and Craig 1913; Minost 1930; Azmi 1934; Lambert 1938), but these were sector studies with no explicit assessment of the degree of inequality.

2. Among the early studies we can mention are Mead (1967) who examined the changes in the distribution of income between 1950 and 1960; Hansen, 1968 who looked at the distributive shares in the agricultural sector during 1897–1961, and Mabro (1974) who assessed, among other things, distributional changes between 1950 and 1965.

3. Holdings of land have been carefully distinguished from ownership of lands. A holding of cultivated land, whether consolidated or fragmented, may be owned by the cultivator, rented or shared in some form of partnership. An ownership is an aggregate consisting of all property of a particular owner. In Egypt, statistics on distribution of holdings and ownerships enumerate individuals, since both holdings and ownerships are registered by individuals, not by families. The difference between holding and ownership depends on the dominance of land lease and sharing, both prevalent in Egypt (Hansen 1991).

4. A broad definition of income would also include income from dairy production and non-agricultural activities.

5. In 2009 the first study that measures inequality of opportunities was published (Hassin 2009)

6. A sample survey undertaken by the Population and Family Planning Board in 1979.

7. A survey carried out by the International Labour Organization (ILO) in 1977.

8. The III index is calculated as the ratio of $\left[\sum_{i=1}^{N}\left|(X-\mathrm{RS}_i)\right|\right]/2$ to $(100-X)$, where X = fixed population interval and equal income-distribution share; RS_i= relative income share of the ith population interval, and N = number of population intervals (that is $N = 5$ for a quintile distribution of the population, $N = 10$ for a decile distribution, and so on).

9. One feddan is equal to 0.42 hectars.

10. Three agrarian reform laws were enacted in the years 1852, 1961 and 1969.

11. No study provided estimates of economy-wide Gini coefficient between 1974/75 and 1981/82, making the developments of income inequality during this period unknown to observers.

12. Also, using various summary measures of inequality, Abdel-Fadil (1975) too showed that there was a slight fall in the overall degree of inequality of the distribution of total consumption between 1958 and 1964.

13. Contrary to the findings in all these studies, Levy, 1986 found some increase in equality in the rural income distribution between 1958/59 and 1964/65, and a slight reduction in the decade ending in 1974/75. On the other hand, Levy, 1986 found that urban areas had an increase in income inequality in the first period, and a decrease in the second.

14. The share of property income is not reported here since it is just the counterpart of the changes in the share of labor, and because it is calculated as a residual (El-Issawy 1981).

References

Abdel-Fadil, Mahmoud. 1975. *Development, Income Distribution and Social Change in Rural Egypt (1952–70)*. Cambridge, UK: Cambridge University Press.

Abdel-Khalek, Gouda, and Robert Tignor, eds. 1982. *The Political Economy of Income Distribution in Egypt*. New York: Holmes and Meiser Publishers.

Adams, Richard H., Jr. 1985. "Development and Structural Change in Rural Egypt, 1952–1982." *World Development* 13 (6): 705–23.

———. 1989. "Worker Remittances and Inequality in Rural Egypt." *Economic Development and Cultural Change* 38 (1): 45–71. http://www.jstor.org/stable/1154160.

———. 1991. "The Effects of International Remittances on Poverty, Inequality, and Development in Rural Egypt." Research Report, no. 86, International Food Policy Research Institute, Washington, DC.

———. 2002. "Nonfarm Income, Inequality, and Land in Rural Egypt." *Economic Development and Cultural Change* 50 (2): 339–63. The University of Chicago Press. http://www.jstor.org/stable/10.1086/321913.

Adams, Richard H., Jr., and Sonia M. Ali. 1996. "The Egyptian Food Subsidy System: Operation and Effects on Income Distribution." *World Development* 24(11): 1777–91.

Ahmad, Iman. 2010. "The Disparity between the Governorates of Egypt in Equitable Distribution of Income and Poverty Levels, in Arabic." Working Paper Series, Faculty of Economics and Political Science.

Alderman, Harold, and Joachim von Braun. 1984. *The Effects of the Egyptian Food Ration and Subsidy System on Income Distribution and Consumption.* Washington, DC: International Food Policy Research Institute (IFPRI).

Azmi, Hamed El Sayed. 1934. "A Study of Agricultural Revenue in Egypt, Rental Value of Agricultural Land, and the Present Incidence of the Land Tax." *I'Egypte Contemporaine* 7 (152): 693–717.

Central Bank of Egypt. 1968. "Changes in the Pattern of Land ownership in UAR (1952–65)." *CBE Economic Review* VIII (3 & 4).

Central Agency for Public Mobilization and Statistics (CAPMAS). 2000. "Household Income, Expenditure and Consumption Survey 1999/2000." CAPMAS, Egypt.

———. 2005. "Household Income, Expenditure and Consumption Survey 2004/05." CAPMAS, Egypt.

———. 2009. "Household Income, Expenditure and Consumption Survey 2008/09." CAPMAS, Egypt.

El-Edel, M. Reda. 1982. "Impact of taxation on Income Distribution: An Exploratory Attempt to Estimate Tax Incidence in Egypt." In *The Political Economy of Income Distribution in Egypt,* edited by Gouda Abdel Khalek and Robert Tignor. New York: Holmes and Meiser Publishers.

El-Issawy, Ibrahim H. 1979. "Distribution, Growth and Development: Some Theoretical Issues and Scientific Observations with Special Reference to Egypt." (In Arabic) in Economic Development and Social Justice in the Modern Thinking, with special reference to Egypt. *Proceedings of the Fourth Annual Conference of Egyptian Economists.*

———. 1982. "Income Distribution and Economic Growth." In *The Political Economy of Income Distribution in Egypt,* edited by Gouda Abdel Khalek and Robert Tignor. New York: Holmes and Meiser Publishers.

El-Kholi, Osman. 1973. "Disparities of Egytpian Personal Income Distribution as Reflected by Family Budget Data." *L'Egypte Contemporaine* LXIV (354), October.

El-Laithy, Heba. 2008. "Non-farm Employment and Inequality in Rural Egypt." Background paper prepared for *"Upper Egypt: Challenges and Priorities for Rural Development."* Washington, DC: World Bank. In 2006 and updated for UEIGP but unpublished.

El-Samman, Ahmad Hamadallah. 1984. "Income Distribution in Rural and Urban Egypt (1952–1981/82)." *L'Egypte Contemporaine.*

Esfehani, Hadi S. 1987. "Growth, Employment and Income Distribution in Egyptian Agriculture, 1964–79." *World Development* 15 (9): 1201–17.

Eshag, E., and M. A. Kamal. 1968. "Agrarian Reform in the UAR (Egypt)." *Bulletin of the Oxford University Institute of Economics and Statistics* 30 (2), May.

Hansen, Bent. 1968. "The Distributive Shares in Egyptian Agriculture, 1987–1961." *International Economic Review* 9 (2): 175–94. http://www.jstore.org/stable/2525473.

———. 1991. *The Political Economy of Poverty, Equity and Growth: Egypt and Turkey.* Oxford: Oxford University Press.

Hansen, Bent, and Samir Radwan. 1982. *Employment Opportunities and Equity in a Changing Economy: Egypt in the 1980s; A Labour Market Approach.* Geneva: ILO.

Hassine, Nadia Belhaj. 2009. "Inequality of Opportunity in Egypt." Conference paper, presented in *Shocks, Vulnerability and Therapy,* ERF 16th Annual Conference, November 7–9.

Jolliffe, Dean, Gaurav Datt, and Manohar Sharma. 2004. "Robust Poverty and Inequality Measurement in Egypt: Correcting for Spatial-price Variation and Sample Design Effects." *Review of Development Economics* 8 (4): 557–72.

Kheir-El-Din, Hanaa, and Heba El-Laithy. 2006. "An Assessment of Growth, Distribution and Poverty in Egypt: 1990/91–2004/05." Working Paper, no. 115, The Egyptian Center for Economic Studies, Cairo, December.

Korayem, Karima. 1978. "Income Distribution between Urban and Rural in Egypt (1952–1975)." (In Arabic), in The Egyptian Economy in Twenty Five Years 1952–1975, *Proceedings of the Third Annual Conference of Egyptian Economists.*

———. 1981. "The Rural-Urban Income Gap in Egypt and Biased Agricultural Pricing Policy." *Social Problems* 28 (4): 417–29. University of California Press. http://www.jstor.org/stable/800055.

———. 1984. "The Income Distribution in Urban Egypt." IBM- Cairo Scientific Center, Egypt, Technical Report no.4, August.

———. 1994. *Poverty and Income Distribution in Egypt.* Third World Forum (Middle East Office), March.

———. 1997. "Egypt's Economic Reform and Structural Adjustment (ERSAP)." Working Paper, No. 19, The Egyptian Center for Economic Studies (ECES), October.

———. 2002. "Pro-Poor Policies in Egypt: Identification and Assessment." *International Journal of Political Economy* 32 (2): 67–96. http://www.jstor.org/stable /40470803.

———. 2008. "Trade Policy in Egypt; Economic and Social Impact." In Institutions and Development in the Arab World, *Proceedings of the 8th Annual Conference of the Arab Association for Economic Research,* edited by Mohamed Samir Mostafa, The Arab Fund for Economic and Social Development.

Lambert, A. 1938. "Divers Modes de Faire Valoir des Terres en Egypte." *1'Egypte Contemporaine,* no. 176 & 177 (Mars-Avril): 181–200.

Levy, Victor. 1986. "The Distributional Impact of Economic Growth and Decline in Egypt." *Middle Eastern Studies* 22 (1): 89–103. http://www.jstor.org/stable/4283098.

Lipton, Michael. 1980. "Migration from Rural Areas of Poor Countries: The Impact on Rural Productivity and Income Distribution." *World Development* 8 (January): 1–24.

Mabro, Robert. 1974. *The Egyptian Economy, 1952–72.* Oxford: Clarendon Press.

Mead, D. 1967. *Growth and Structural Change in the Egyptian Economy.* New Haven: Economic Growth Center, Yale University.

Minost, E. 1930. "Essai sur la Revenue Agricole de l'Egypte." *l'Egypte Contemporaine* 6 (123): 535–83.

Mohie-Eldin, Amr. 1980. Urban Income Distribution. Mimeographed, Cairo.

———. 1982. "The Development of the Share of Agricultural Wage Labor in the National Income of Egypt." In *The Political Economy of Income Distribution in Egypt,* edited by Gouda Abdel Khalek and Robert Tignor. New York: Holmes and Meiser Publishers.

Radwan, Samir. 1977. *Agrarian Reform and Rural Poverty, Egypt, 1952–1975.* Geneva: International Labor Office.

Radwan, Samir, and Eddy Lee. 1986. *Agrarian Change in Egypt; an Anatomy of Rural Poverty.* London: Croom Helm.

Willcocks, W. 1899. *Egyptian Irrigation.* 2nd ed. London: E. and F. N. Spon; New York: Spon and Chamberlain.

Willcocks, W., and J. T. Craig. 1913. *Egyptian Irrigation*. 3rd ed. 2 vols. London: E. and F. N. Spon; New York: Spon and Chamberlain.

World Bank. 1989. "Arab Republic of Egypt: A Study on Poverty and the Distribution of Income." A draft report of the country operations Division, CD111, EMENA, January 5.

———. 1991. *Alleviating Poverty during Structural Adjustment*. Washington, DC: World Bank.

———.2002. "Arab Republic of Egypt: Poverty Reduction in Egypt Diagnosis and Strategy." Vol. 1. Main Report, World Bank, Washington, DC.

———. 2007. "Arab Republic of Egypt: Poverty Assessment Update." Vol. 1. Main Report, World Bank, Washington, DC. https://openknowledge.worldbank.org/handle /10986/7642.

———. 2011, *Arab Republic of Egypt: Poverty in Egypt 2008–09: Withstanding the Global Economic Crisis*. Washington, DC: World Bank.

Yitzhaki, Shlomo. 1990. "On the Effect of Subsidies to Basic Food Commodities in Egypt." *Oxford Economic Papers New Series* 42 (4): 772–92. Oxford University Press. http://www.jstor.org/stable/266312.

Zaytoun, Mohaya A. 1982. "Income Distribution in Egyptian Agriculture and its Main Determinants." In *The Political Economy of Income Distribution in Egypt*, edited Gouda Abdel Khalek and Robert Tignor. New York: Holmes and Meiser Publishers.

CHAPTER 2

Spatial Inequality

Branko Milanovic

Introduction

This part looks at the Arab Republic of Egypt's inequality in the global context and spatial inequality across urban and rural areas and across Egypt's governorates. Section 1 compares the values of inequality for Egypt to those of similar countries across the world and across the Middle East and North Africa region. Sections 2 and 3 describe and analyse, respectively, the urban-rural gap (mean income in the urban areas vs. mean income in the rural areas) and interpersonal inequalities in urban and rural areas. This is done for 2005, the year for which the data from the household survey are available in full. This static picture is complemented by the analysis in section 3 where we focus on the changes that have occurred over the period 2005–09. For 2009, we use a random sample (25 percent) drawn from the full household survey for that year, given that the full survey data are not available. Finally, section 4 looks at convergence or divergence of mean urban and rural governorate incomes.

We focus on spatial inequality because it is considered to be one of the main causes of overall interpersonal inequality in Egypt. Geographical pockets of poverty are associated with "poverty traps," the situations where individuals—by being born and raised in certain areas—are de facto excluded from enjoying improvements of income and welfare that may occur elsewhere. Poverty and inequality are thus perpetuated.

We shall however find that this picture is more nuanced. The urban-rural gap in Egypt is indeed large but is, to a significant extent, driven by the gap that exists between the four metropolitan areas and the rest of the country. The conventionally measured urban-rural gap is reduced by about a third if we measure the gap only in "mixed" governorates (such that they contain both urban and rural areas). As is often the case, urban inequality (measured across all urban areas) as well as inequality in urban parts of individual governorates is greater than rural inequality. Metropolitan areas stand out by their greater inequality, but Cairo, for example, is not more unequal than similar-sized cities elsewhere in the developing world.

The overall picture of interpersonal inequality in Egypt is both (i) muted compared to what one might have expected, particularly if contrasted with the view that the recent political changes have been brought about by rising inequality, and (ii) shows little variation during the past decade: the countrywide Gini was in the range between 33 and 35 Gini points. These facts have stimulated more research into other ways in which inequality might affect public perceptions, or have raised some questions about survey's reliability in covering high incomes (see part on facts and perceptions of inequality).

Egypt Inequality in the Global Context

Between 2005 and 2009, the overall income Gini for Egypt decreased from 34.6 to 33.1. The decrease is not statistically significant (at 5 percent level), and thus we can basically speak of an unchanged level of income inequality around 33–35 Gini points. This is a level very similar to that of the developed European Organisation for Economic Co-operation and Development (OECD) members. It is significantly lower than income inequality in the United States (which exceeds 40), and is likewise lower than inequality in most countries that are close to Egypt in terms of gross domestic product (GDP) per capita. For example, in 2009, Georgia, Guatemala, and China that, according to GDP per capita (measured in purchasing power parities [PPPs] terms), are around Egypt's income level had all higher inequality: Guatemala had an income Gini of 57, Georgia a consumption Gini of 39, and China an income Gini of 47.

The situation of Egypt, however, is not so special when it is compared with other Arab countries for which we have the data. Arab countries are distinguished by relatively low inequality (this may not be however the case for the countries for which we lack data, as for example Saudi Arabia). Table 2.1 shows some illustrative results. None of the countries shows an outstanding level of inequality. Their Ginis range between around 33 and 40, and Egypt's inequality is the lowest. Although we cannot be sure about the rankings because the welfare concepts and survey methodologies differ, there is no evidence that Egypt's inequality level is any different from what is found in other Arab countries.

Table 2.1 Income and Expenditure Ginis in Arab Countries (on Per Capita Basis)

	Year	Welfare concept	Gini
Morocco	2007	Expenditures	40.7
Jordan	2002	Expenditures	38.6
Yemen	2008	Expenditures	37.4
Iraq	2008	Income	36.0
Syria	2004	Expenditures	35.7
Sudan	2009	Expenditures	34.4
Egypt, Arab Rep.	2009	Income	33.1

Source: Egypt: HIECS 2009.
Note: Countries ranked by Gini.

Figure 2.1 Egyptian Gini within Global Distribution of Ginis, 2008–09

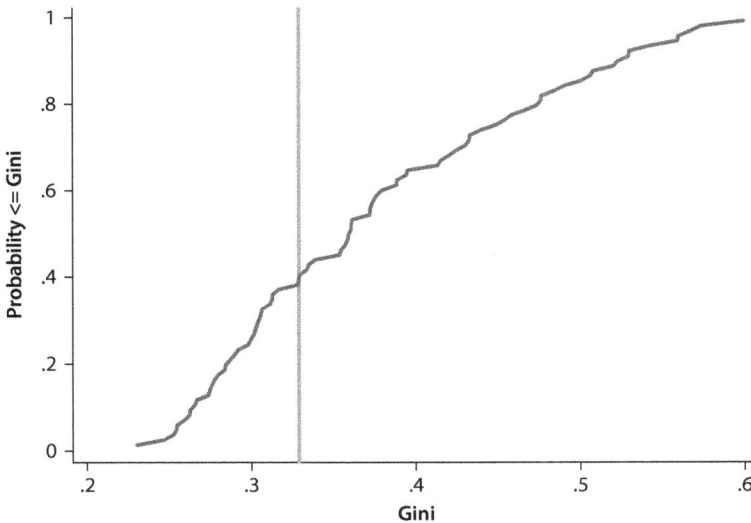

Source: All the Ginis database, HIECS 2009.

Using the most recent 2009 data for Egypt, we can also situate Egypt within the international inequality spectrum around the same year. As figure 2.1 shows, if we plot a cumulative worldwide distribution of country Ginis, Egypt's inequality would be around the 40th percentile (see the vertical line). In other words, Egypt's inequality is below median international inequality.

In figure 2.2, we plot the same Gini from around 2008–09 against GDP per capita in the same year. We have data from 88 countries, based on comparable or same definitions of income or expenditures, and the same definition of household per capita Gini. As is often the case in cross-sectional results, inequality is negatively associated with GDP per capita. Egypt's Gini lies clearly below the regression line, that is, it is (again) relatively low for its income level.

In figure 2.3, we contrast Egyptian income distribution to that of several selected countries. We aim to show where in the global income distributions are individuals situated at different percentiles of Egyptian income distribution. The horizontal axis shows percentiles of national income distributions, ranging from 1 to 100, and the vertical axis shows their positions in the global income distribution, ranging also from 1 to 100. Thus, for example, the bottom US percentile is at the 55th global percentile, indicating that the poorest Americans are better off than more than one-half of world population. The poorest Egyptians are at the 15th global income percentile, and each richer Egyptian percentile of course stands higher in the global income distribution. Egyptians at the median of national income distribution are also around the median of the global income distribution. The richest 1 percent of Egyptians are at the 92nd global percentile.

We can easily compare the positions of various Egyptian percentiles with that of people from other countries. It is thus remarkable that the poorest people in

Figure 2.2 Gini and GDP Per Capita, 2008–09

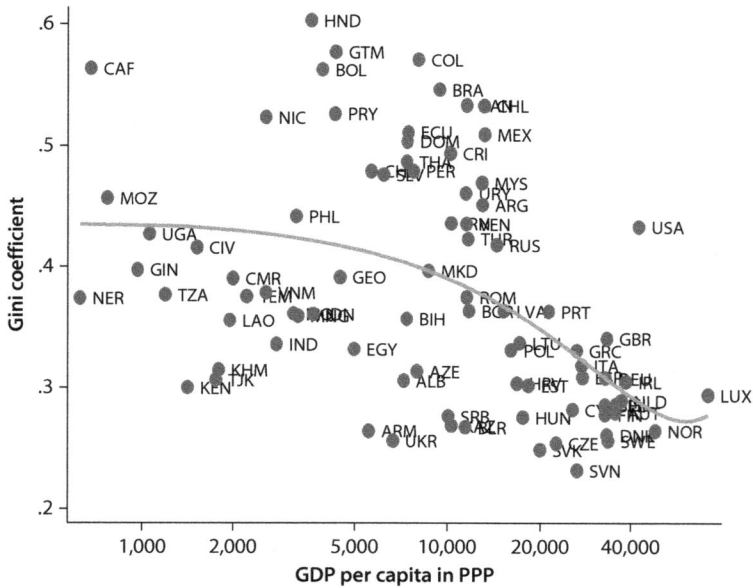

Source: All the Ginis database and World Development Indicators.
Note: GDP = gross domestic product; PPP = purchasing power parity.

Figure 2.3 Egyptian Income Distribution Compared to that of Selected Countries and the World

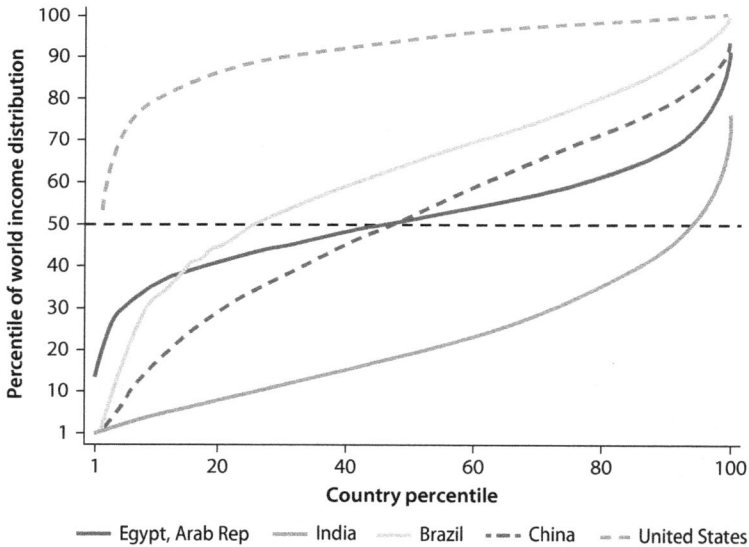

Source: World Income Distribution (WYD) database, benchmark year 2009; HIECS 2009.

Egypt are not as destitute as those in India, China, and Brazil. In effect, up to the 10th percentile, people in Egypt are better off than similarly placed people in Brazil; up to the 50th national percentile, they are better off than similarly placed people in China, and throughout the income distribution Egypt dominates India. This means that at any given point of the income distribution, people in Egypt are better off than similar people in India. Egypt's distribution thus displays the first-order stochastic dominance.

The relationship between incomes in China and Egypt is interesting. After the median, Chinese incomes exceed those of similarly placed Egyptians. However, at the very top of the income distribution, richest 1 percent of Egyptians catch up with the richest 1 percent of the Chinese.

Finally, and not surprisingly, in a similar way that Egypt shows first-order dominance over India, so does the United States first-order dominates Egypt. Around 60 percent of Egyptians live at the income levels inferior to that of the poorest 1 percent of Americans. Even upper middle income Egyptians barely reach the level of income enjoyed by the lower-middle-income population in the United States. This is of course not surprising because the main determinant of one's overall position in the global income distribution is the mean income of his/her country. Thus, disposable mean per capita household income in the United States is 25,500 international dollars while it is only 2,000 in Egypt (the ratio is more than 12 to 1). Measured by GDP per capita in international dollars, the gap in 2008 exceeds 8 to 1 (43,000 against 5,000). Thus, even if the two distributions were exactly the same, we would expect to find at any point of national income distribution an American to be 8 to 12 times richer than an equivalent Egyptian.

Urban-Rural Gap in Egypt in 2005

At first sight, the urban/rural gap in Egypt appears quite deep. The average per capita urban income is 67 percent higher than the average rural income (see table 2.2). Among the people who are included in the top 1 percent (assessed by their household per capita income) 93 percent live in urban areas; among the top 10 percent, their share is still an overwhelming 81 percent. Since the overall

Table 2.2 Urban-rural Divide in Egypt (All Governorates)

	Urban	Rural	Overall
Mean (normalized) per capita income	1.294	0.775	1
Population share (in %)	43.4	56.6	100
Share of total income (in %)	56.1	43.9	100
Inequality (Gini)	37.5 (0.3)	26.5 (0.2)	34.6 (0-2)
Inequality (Theil 0 or mean log deviation)	23.2 (0.6)	11.6 (0.5)	19.9 (0-5)
Inequality (Theil 1 or Theil entropy index)	28.6 (0.8)	13.3 (0.7)	25.2 (0-6)

Source: HIECS 2005.
Note: Income normalized by the mean income for Egypt. Standard errors of inequality coefficients between brackets.

Inside Inequality in the Arab Republic of Egypt • http://dx.doi.org/10.1596/978-1-4648-0198-3

Figure 2.4 The Percentage Shares of Urban and Rural Populations in Ten Income Deciles

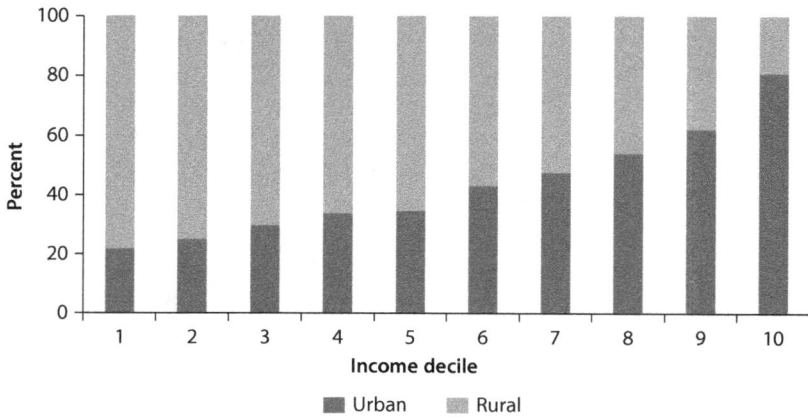

Source: HIECS 2005.

share of the urban population is only 43 percent, it is clear that the urban population is overrepresented among the rich. For example, an urban citizen has 17
times greater probability to be part of the top percentile than a person living in
rural areas (93/43 divided by 7/57). Figure 2.4 illustrates the fact of the steadily
increasing share of the urban population as the level of income (income decile)
increases. The top and the bottom deciles are almost exact mirror images of each
other: while in the bottom decile, the urban population accounts for only 22 percent of people, in the top decile its share is 81 percent.

The urban-rural divide also contributes strongly to the overall inequality. Out
of the total (all-Egypt) Gini coefficient of 36.4 points, 12.75 points (or more
than 1/3) is explained just by the difference in mean incomes between urban and
rural areas. If we use Theil's inequality measures, the share is somewhat less but
is still between one-sixth and one-seventh (see table 2.3).

However, a more careful look at the divide reveals a somewhat different picture. If we focus on the rural-urban divide only in the governorates where both
urban and rural settlements exist (for simplicity, we call them "mixed governorates"), it emerges that the difference in average incomes is significantly less:
Instead of a 67 percent gap, the gap is now only 41 percent. Table 2.4 repro-
duces table 2.2 but focuses only on mixed governorates (23 out of 27). An obvious implication is that almost 40 percent of the observed urban/rural gap is not

Table 2.3 Importance of the "Between" (Rural/Urban) Component in Overall Inequality

	Between component	Between component as % of total inequality
Gini	12.75	35.8
Theil (0)	3.3	16.6
Theil (1)	3.3	13.1

Source: HIECS 2005.

Table 2.4 Urban-Rural Divide in Egypt in Mixed Governorates, 2005

	Urban	Rural	Overall
Mean (normalized) per capita income	1.256	0.889	1
Population share (in %)	30.3	69.7	100
Share of total income (in %)	38.1	61.9	100
Inequality (Gini)	33.3 (0.4)	26.5 (0.2)	34.6 (0.2)
Inequality (Theil 0 or mean log deviation)	18.3 (0.5)	11.6 (0.5)	19.9 (0.5)
Inequality (Theil 1 or Theil entropy index)	21.6 (0.6)	13.3 (0.7)	25.2 (0.7)

Source: HIECS 2005.

Note: Income normalized by the mean income for Egypt. Standard errors of inequality coefficients between brackets.

Figure 2.5 Urban-Rural Income Gap by Governorate

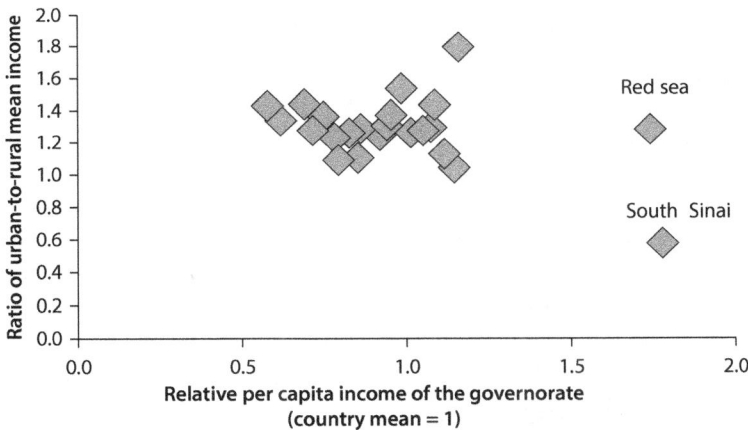

Source: World Bank data.

really an urban/rural gap but rather a geographical gap where the metropolitan governorates are simply a richer part of the country.

Among the governorates where both the rural and urban population live, there is no tendency for the richer governorates to display a wider urban/rural gap. This is clear from figure 2.5. Among the governorates whose average income ranges between 0.6 and 1.2 of the countrywide mean, the urban/rural ratio is a little over 1.2 with no clear tendency up or down, and in the two much richer governorates (Red Sea and South Sinai), the gap is either 1.3 or, rather unexpectedly, 0.6 (that is, rural areas are richer in South Sinai!). But the population importance of these two governorates is tiny: Together they account for 0.6 percent of the population living in mixed governorates. There is also no clear relationship between urban/rural gap (in the mixed governorates) and population size of the governorate (figure 2.6).

Figure 2.6 Urban-Rural Income Gap by Population Size of Governorate

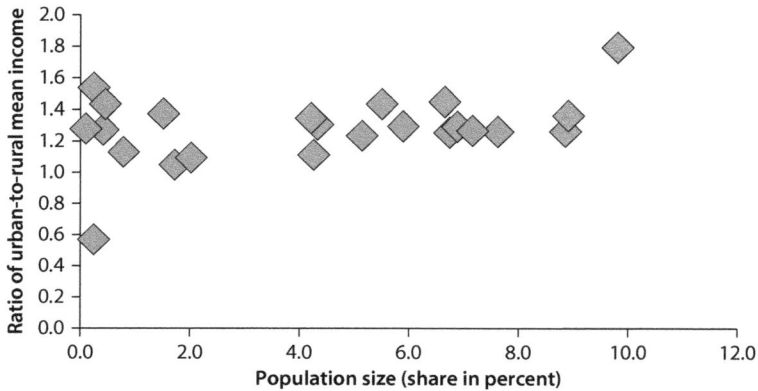

Source: HIECS 2005.
Note: Population size is total population residing in governorates (according to household survey data) as percentage of total Egyptian population living in "mixed governorates."

Interpersonal Inequality in Rural and Urban Areas

Is Interpersonal Inequality in Urban Areas Greater than in Rural?

It is often the case that inequality in urban areas exceeds inequality in rural areas. For example, in Indonesia 2008, urban consumption Gini is 38 while the rural consumption Gini is 28, in the Philippines 2009, urban consumption Gini is 41, equivalent rural Gini 38. China, due to its communist legacy as well as the fact that both rural and urban areas surveys cover only the registered (not resident) populations living in the two areas, is one of the few countries where urban inequality is less than rural. Egypt however is not an exception. As shown in table 2.2, the urban income Gini is 37.5 and the rural income Gini is more than 10 Gini points lower (26.4); the difference is statistically highly significant (see the standard errors in table 2.2).

Greater inequality in urban areas is also obvious from figure 2.7 where a familiar box-and-whiskers diagram shows that both tails of the income distribution are more elongated in urban areas. There are both more extremely rich and poor people in the urban areas, and, as we have seen before, the mean and the median (indicated by the horizontal line within the box) are greater in the urban areas.

If we disaggregate these data by governorate, the results are unchanged. The average unweighted mean Gini in urban areas is 29.9, and in rural areas it is 25.7 (see table 2.5). Even if we omit the metropolitan governorates (Cairo, Alexandria, Port Said, and Suez) that are generally more unequal,[1] the gap still persists (28.6 vs. 25.7). The difference is 3 Gini points which is about one standard deviation of either urban or rural Ginis (by governorate).

Figure 2.8 shows the distribution of urban and rural governorates' Ginis. As already stressed, urban Ginis tend to be higher and their density function is shifted more to the right than the density function of the rural Ginis. The distribution of urban Ginis is fairly close to symmetrical with both the mean and the

Figure 2.7 A Summary Look at Urban and Rural Income Distributions

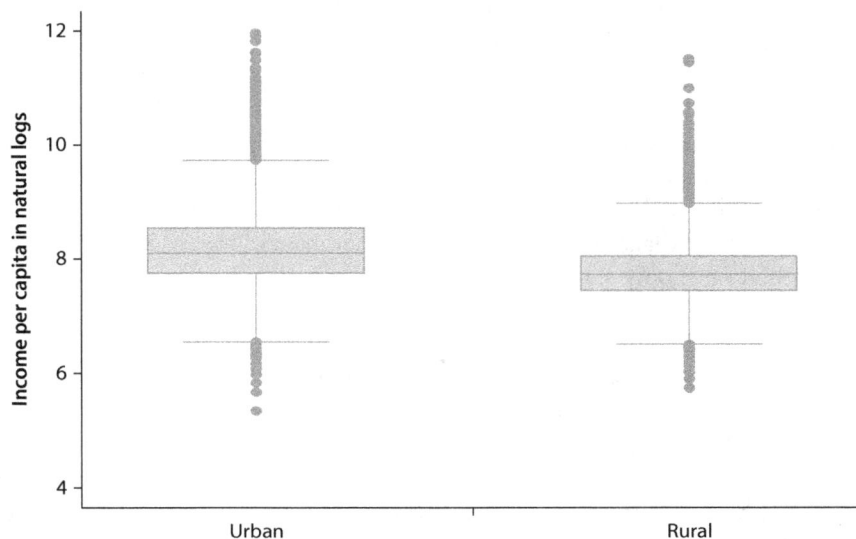

Source: HIECS 2005.

Table 2.5 Gini in Urban and Rural Areas (Governorates)

	Urban areas	Rural areas	Difference
Unweighted mean Gini	29.9	25.7	4.2
Unweighted mean Gini in mixed governorates	28.7	25.7	3.0

Source: HIECS 2005.

Figure 2.8 Distribution of Urban and Rural Gini Coefficients (by Governorate)

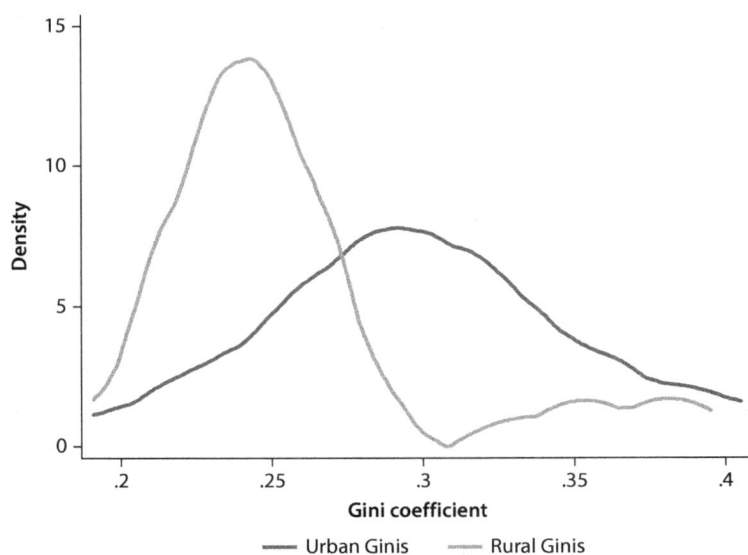

Source: HIECS 2005.

Inside Inequality in the Arab Republic of Egypt • http://dx.doi.org/10.1596/978-1-4648-0198-3

median around 30. The distribution of rural Ginis is skewed to the right (there are several atypically high rural Ginis), but the bulk of rural Ginis are located around the low Gini value of 25. However, there is some overlap: There are Ginis in rural governorates that are as high or higher than the urban Ginis in the same governorates. The rural Ginis in Luxor and the Frontier governorates are all higher than the corresponding urban Ginis (but again their populations are very small).

The next question that can be asked is whether urban governorates with high Ginis also exhibit high rural Ginis. This however is not the case: As figure 2.9 shows, the scatter diagram seems close to random and the linear correlation between the two is only +0.11 (and not significantly different from 0).

What "Explains" Urban and Rural Inequality?

In figure 2.10 (panels a and b), we look at urban and rural Ginis in function of both the level of income in urban and rural parts of the governorate, and population size. A look at the graphs suffices to show that the association between average per capita income by governorate (rural and urban) and the Gini coefficient (rural and urban) is very weak. In other words, the income level and inequality are not obviously associated.

Figure 2.9 Absence of Correlation between Urban and Rural Ginis in the Same Governorates

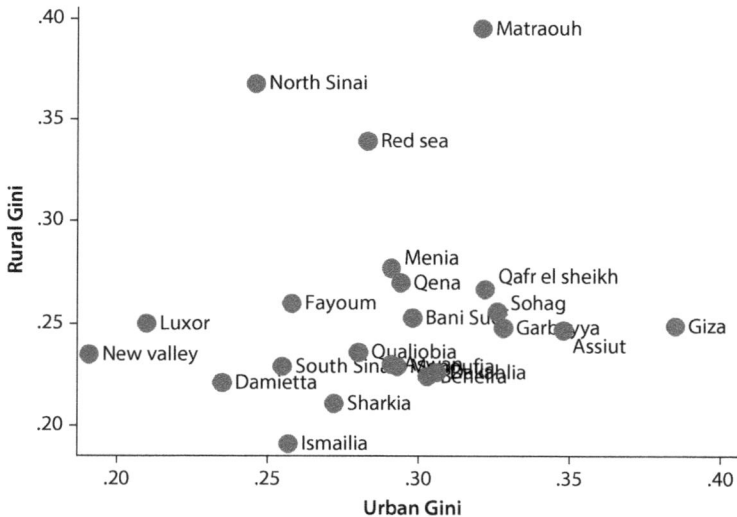

Source: HIECS 2005.

Only slightly stronger is the correlation between population size and inequality except for urban Ginis where large population sizes in the metropolitan governorates (in particular Cairo), drive a positive relationship. In effect, when we run a simple regression for urban Gini on mean per capita income in the urban governorates and size of urban population, the

Figure 2.10 Gini in Urban and Rural Areas Against Average Incomes (with Dots Reflecting Population Sizes)

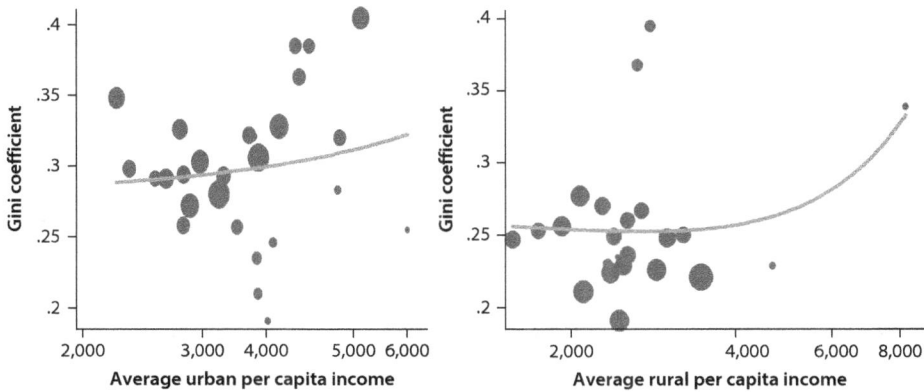

Source: HIECS 2005.

coefficient on population is positive and statistically significant with the *t*-value of 4.4 (the coefficient on income is not statistically significant). When we drop four metropolitan governorates, the size and the significance of the coefficient on population decreases, but still remains statistically significant (*t* value of 3.90).[2]

Thus, while rural inequality does not exhibit any obvious correlation with mean income or population size, urban inequality seems to be higher in more populous areas. (Note that the regression is not population weighted so the importance of Cairo in the regression is the same as of any other urban governorate).

Evolution of Real Incomes and Inequality between 2005 and 2009

As table 2.6 makes clear, total real per capita income, as measured by household surveys, decreased in Egypt between 2005 and 2009 by 8.7 percent.[3] The decrease affected both urban and rural areas, although the decline was more severe in the former. Consequently, the urban/rural gap decreased somewhat from its 2005 value of 1.67 to 1.61.

Table 2.6 Real Per Capita Income, 2000–09

In 2005 Egyptian pounds per year

	2005	2009	% change 2005–2009
Urban	3,962	3,602	−9.1
Rural	2,372	2,237	−5.7
Total	3,061	2,796	−8.7

Source: HIECS 2005, 2009.

Table 2.7 shows the real per capita income change by governorate and by its urban and rural parts. Declines in real income have been pervasive. In urban areas, decreases were recorded in 16 out of 27 governorates; in rural governorates, in even more: 18 of 23. The difference however has been that in the urban areas, the real income decline was particularly large in very populous areas, thus driving down the overall change in urban areas. As seen in table 2.6, the mean real income in Cairo went down by a whopping 14 percent, and in Alexandria by even more (16 percent). Obviously, real income is a reflection of changes in nominal magnitudes deflated by the consumer cost of living. High increase in

Table 2.7 Real Income Change between 2005 and 2009, by Governorate and Urban/Rural Area

Amounts in real 2005 Egyptian pounds per capita

	Urban areas			Rural areas		
	2005	*2009*	*2009 level[a]*	*2005*	*2009*	*2009 level[a]*
Cairo	5,132	4,434	0.86			
Alexandra	4,110	3,448	0.84			
Port Said	4,164	4,073	0.98			
Suez	4,777	4,855	1.02			
Domiat	3,609	4,273	1.18	3,457	3,113	0.90
Dakahlia	3,630	3,291	0.91	2,870	2,730	0.95
Sharkya	2,875	2,788	0.97	2,109	2,195	1.04
Kaliobia	3,176	3,404	1.07	2,545	2,234	0.88
Kafr el-sheikh	3,517	3,416	0.97	2,693	2,703	1.00
Gharbia	3,893	3,581	0.92	3,001	2,585	0.86
Menofia	3,226	3,310	1.03	2,498	2,403	0.96
Behira	2,977	2,514	0.84	2,364	2,278	0.96
Ismailia	3,376	4,220	1.25	2,456	3,925	1.60
Giza	4,304	3,637	0.85	2,396	2,080	0.87
Bani-souwayf	2,343	2,076	0.89	1,744	1,721	0.99
Fayom	2,811	2,189	0.78	2,541	1,878	0.74
Menia	2,653	3,209	1.21	2,079	2,104	1.01
Asyout	2,245	2,618	1.17	1,566	1,486	0.95
Souhag	2,781	2,093	0.75	1,927	1,742	0.90
Qena	2,815	2,896	1.03	2,283	2,032	0.89
Aswan	2,557	2,491	0.97	2,336	2,194	0.94
Louxor	3,624	4,041	1.12	3,212	2,915	0.91
Red-sea	4,744	4,356	0.92	8,197	2,394	0.29
New valley	3,744	3,437	0.92	2,434	3,274	1.34
Matrouh	3,567	3,807	1.07	2,796	2,563	0.92
North Sinai	3,810	2,563	0.67	2,650	2,054	0.78
South Sinai	6,006	15,019	2.50	4,676	3,858	0.83

Source: HIECS 2005 and 2009.
a. Year 2005=1.

the food prices, driving consumer price index (CPI) up, and nominal incomes which failed to keep the pace, are possibly one of the reasons for these sharp real income declines.

Urban Areas

It is interesting to see whether real declines in the 2005–09 period were associated with 2005 income level, population size, and inequality as measured by the Gini coefficient. The results of regressions are shown in table 2.8. The dependent variable is the ratio between 2009 and 2005 real per capita income by governorate (1 implying that there was neither growth nor decline). For the urban areas, there is only a mild indication that richer areas (in 2005) were able to maintain their position better: Each 100 pounds of higher per capita income in 2005 is associated with a 2 percent higher per capita income level in 2009 (compared to its 2005 level). Since real mean per capita incomes declined everywhere, it means in reality that, for each 100 pounds, the decline was 2 percent smaller. But, on the other hand, more populous and more unequal urban areas are associated with larger real income drops between the two years.

Simplifying the matters slightly, we can now see that the overall large declines in real incomes registered in Cairo and Alexandria were associated with two negative factors (high inequality in both, and high population shares), whereas their relatively high-income level slowed down the decline. It is difficult without further analysis to make hypotheses about the factors that were responsible for these developments, particularly since the sample is small (27 urban governorates) and neither population size nor inequality are statistically significant at conventional levels.

To investigate this further, we look at income change by income decile in urban areas. In principle, the analysis could be conducted for each individual urban governorate (that is, each urban governorate could be divided into 10 income deciles according to per capita income in 2005). Yet, such

Table 2.8 Factors Associated with Real Income Decline between 2005 and 2009, by Governorate

Dependent variable: ratio of 2009 to 2005 real per capita income

	Urban areas	Rural areas
Real per capita income in 2005	0.0002** (0.007)	−0.0001** (0.000)
Gini coefficient in 2005	−0.712 (0.63)	−2.164** (0.006)
Population in 2005	−0.00002 (0.20)	−0.00003* (0.013)
Constant	0.6103 (0.22)	1.954** (0.00)
R^2 adjusted	0.24 (3.7)	0.59 (11.4)
N (governorates)	27	23

Source: HIECS 2005 and HIECS 2009.
Note: p values between brackets. ** (*) = 1% (5%) statistical significance.

an analysis would be both cumbersome and statistically suspicious since either representativeness (particularly of the 2009 survey) cannot be guaranteed at such level of disaggregation, and probably more importantly, in some cases such income deciles would consist of relatively few households. Therefore, we do this type of distributional analysis only for Egypt as a whole and, because of its economic and political importance (and large sample size), for Cairo.

Figure 2.11 shows that real income in 2009 was lower at every decile of urban income distribution and also that, for Egypt as a whole, the decline was more severe for upper income deciles. While the poorest deciles lost around 5 percent in real terms, the very top decile lost 12 percent. There is an almost monotonic relationship such that there is a greater percentage decline in real incomes as income decile rises. The recession was thus "pro-poor" in the urban areas. The situation slightly differs in Cairo only when it comes to the top decile which bucks this tendency, and whose loss was less that the relative loss of several preceding deciles. It is noticeable also that, at every point of the income distribution, the drop in real incomes in Cairo was greater than in urban Egypt overall.

Several conclusions can be made at this stage regarding the evolution of urban real income between 2005 and 2009: (i) It has declined significantly (by about 9 percent), (ii) the declines were sharper among the richest deciles with an apparent exception of Cairo where the top decile did lose but not as much as some lower deciles, and (iii) the average-income decline was positively associated with 2005 level of inequality and urban population size, but negatively with mean income.

Figure 2.11 Ratio of 2009 to 2005 Real Per Capita Income for Urban and Rural Income Deciles

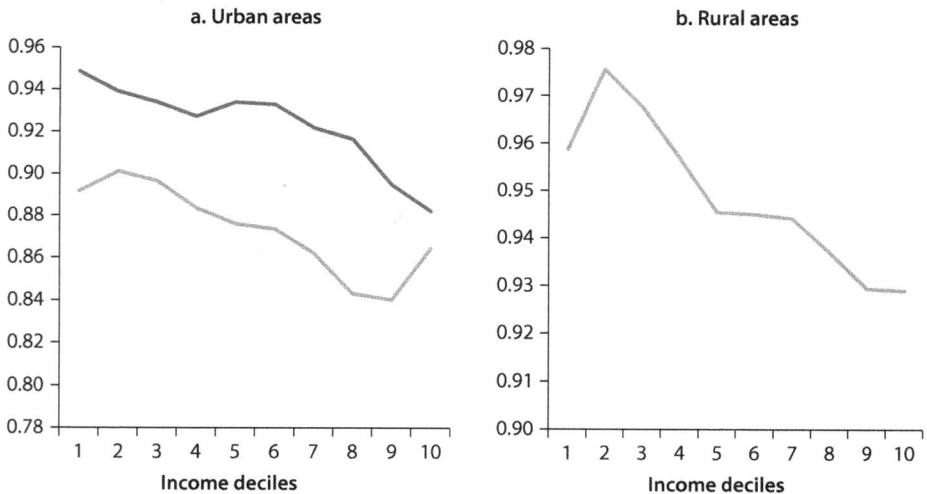

Source: HIECS 2005 and 2009.

Table 2.9 Gini Coefficients in Urban and Rural Areas

Income per capita

	2005	*2009*	*Gini point change*
Urban	37.5 (0.3)	36.3 (0.6)	−1.2
Rural	26.5 (0.2)	25.7 (0.6)	−0.8
All Egypt	34.6 (0.2)	33.0 (0.5)	−1.6
(Cairo)	40.5 (0.8)	39.7 (1.1)	−0.8

Source: HIECS 2005 and 2009.
Note: Standard errors between brackets.

Rural Areas

The factors associated with real income decline in rural areas were statistically less ambiguous than in the case of urban areas: Higher 2005 real per capita income, greater inequality, and greater population were all statistically significantly associated with declines in real income. It is therefore the richer, more populous, and more unequal rural governorates that lost more than the others (see table 2.8). The distribution analysis for rural regions shows, similar to what we found for urban regions, that the declines were more serious for higher-income deciles (figure 2.11). The top two deciles lost each about 7 percent of real per capita income while the bottom rural deciles managed a loss of between 2 and 4 percent. Again, the recession could be said to have been "pro-poor."

An obvious implication of our finding is that, while income declines were pervasive (across most governorates) since they were more severe for the top rural and income deciles, we would expect to find reduction in inequality in both areas. This is indeed the case (see table 2.9): Urban Gini (calculated across all individuals living in urban areas) has decreased by 1.2 and rural Gini by 0.8 points. The overall Gini has declined by more (1.6 Gini points), driven in addition by the declining urban-rural income gap.

Income Convergence or Divergence within Urban and Rural Governorates

But did the gap between governorates decline too? We now ask whether urban and rural governorates' mean incomes have within each subgroup converged or diverged, that is, whether urban governorates' incomes have become more or less similar to each other. This is called Concept 1 inequality which is technically equal to a Gini coefficient calculated across mean governorates' (urban or rural) incomes. Table 2.10 shows the results in the first two lines. Consider first the urban governorates. Urban mean incomes have diverged as reflected in significant increase in the unweighted Gini calculated across their mean incomes. This is not surprising because we have seen before that the declines in real incomes have been less for richer urban governorates.

Table 2.10 Three Concepts of Inequality Applied to Urban and Rural Governorates

	2005	2009
Concept 1 inequality		
(1) Urban	13.5 (1.6)	21.7 (0.6)
(2) Rural	18.7 (5.2)	13.7 (1.8)
Concept 2 inequality =		
between component		
(3) Urban	13.1 (1.7)	15.4 (2.6)
(4) Rural	16.1 (5.0)	14.7 (2.0)
Concept 3 inequality		
(5) Overall urban Gini	37.5 (0.3)	36.3 (0.7)
(6) Overall rural Gini	26.5 (0.2)	25.6 (0.5)
Within component (Concept 3–		
Concept 2)		
Urban=(5)–(3)	24.4	20.9
Rural=(6)–(4)	10.4	10.9

Source: HIECS 2005 and 2009.
Note: Standard errors between brackets. Concept 3 inequality from table 2.9.

The population-weighted measure of divergence Concept 2 Gini which is obtained as a population-weighted Gini index calculated across mean governorates' urban incomes also increased (see line 3, table 2.10), although by much less. We can decompose the overall inequality calculated across individuals in urban areas into the between- and within components.[4] The between component is equal to inequality that would exist if everybody in each governorate would have the mean income of that governorate. It is thus equal to the Concept 2 inequality. The within component is simply obtained as the residual, the difference between the overall interpersonal inequality and Concept 2. As can be seen, the within component in urban governorates has gone down by more than 3 Gini points. In short, this means that while inequality within urban governorates has decreased, urban parts of the governorates have become more dissimilar between themselves (in terms of mean incomes).

When we look at rural governorates, we notice a rather fast convergence in mean unweighted incomes (Concept 1 Gini), and a milder convergence in terms of population-weighted Gini (Concept 2). The overall Gini across all individuals living in rural governorates has declined from 26.5 to 25.6 (see line 6, table 2.10), and the within component has thus slightly gone up. Overall, the changes that we observe across both people living in rural governorates and mean incomes across rural governorates are minor, and not even statistically significant. The same could be said for the Concept 3 (overall inequality) change in the urban governorates, but somewhat less so for other changes in the urban governorates where we note a divergence in mean incomes and the shrinking of interpersonal income distributions within governorates. If these two trends were to continue, they would imply that the mean urban incomes by governorate would become more and more dissimilar, while distributions within each governorate's urban areas would shrink. Such an evolution can be

Figure 2.12 Distribution of Population by Household Per Capita Income in the Poorest and Richest Urban Governorate, 2009

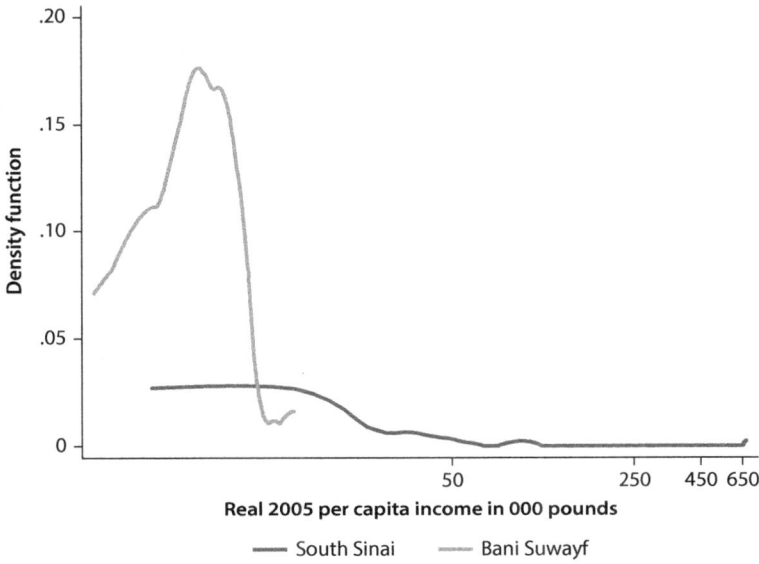

Real 2005 per capita income in 000 pounds

——— South Sinai   ——— Bani Suwayf

Source: HIECS 2005.

depicted by looking at the contrast that currently exists between the distributions in the richest and the poorest urban governorates: As figure 2.12 shows, the overlap between the two distributions is minimal.

Conclusions

Geographical or horizontal inequalities between urban and rural areas are one of the main contributory factors to overall inequality in many countries of the world. Egypt is not an exception, although we find that inequalities are not huge by international standards, and that they are even less so if we compare urban and rural inequalities within the same governorates. The gap is more geographical: It is between the four main Egyptian cities, and the rest of the country, than properly urban-rural. Interpersonal inequality in the urban area (as a whole) is significantly greater than interpersonal inequality in the rural area (as a whole). Similarly, within each governorate, interpersonal inequality in its urban parts (average Gini of about 30) is greater than interpersonal inequality in rural parts (average Gini of 26). This is also not an uncommon feature: Urban incomes tend to be more dispersed reflecting greater variety of population and skills in urban areas. Between 2005 and 2009, the changes in both the gap and inequality have been modest. The urban-rural gap decreased somewhat because the average urban income (as estimated from household surveys) decreased more in real terms than the average rural income. Urban and rural inequalities hardly changed at all. The only notable feature was the divergence of urban governorates' average incomes.

Inside Inequality in the Arab Republic of Egypt • http://dx.doi.org/10.1596/978-1-4648-0198-3

Notes

1. The most unequal of all governorates is, not surprisingly, Cairo with a Gini of 40.5. The second most unequal in Alexandria with a Gini of 38.5. The Gini numbers for Cairo are in line with other large international metropolitan areas: Manila's Gini is 42, Bangkok's 41, and Kuala Lumpur's (income based) 41.

2. These are very tentative results due to the small number of observations over which they are run (27 governorates).

3. This differs from National accounts data that show real GDP per capita to be 14 percent higher in 2009 than in 2005 (World Development Indicators 2012). An underestimation of top incomes in household surveys in 2009 is possible.

4. The within component here includes both the standard within component from the Gini decomposition and the so-called overlap term.

CHAPTER 3

Facts and Perceptions of Inequality

Paolo Verme

Introduction

Press coverage of the Egyptian revolution, both local and international, makes frequent use of the word "inequality" to describe one of the factors that generated discontent. During the current transitional phase, two of the themes that are inspiring popular debates and political parties in the making are the questions of social justice and equality. The general perception is that social injustice and a somehow unequal distribution of resources were deep-rooted phenomena under the Mubarak regime and that these factors contributed to explain the eruption of social discontent. This perception is not only conveyed by media and popular debates but also by intellectuals and academics. The Egyptian Center for Economic Studies (ECES), for example, argued that "Social inequality and inadequate human development coupled with the lack of political reforms have been among the main factors that led to the outbreak of the revolution" (p. 7, ECES, Policy Viewpoint, May, 2011). The term "inequality" as used by the press is a rather loose term that may be associated with inequalities of various kinds such as social, status, and access to services and resources or opportunities more in general. But in many people's mind the term "inequality" refers to inequality of wealth or incomes.

One of the puzzling aspects of this malaise about inequality is that the measurement of monetary inequality in the Arab Republic of Egypt by means of household surveys does not seem to match perceptions. According to both official government figures and the World Bank, the Gini coefficient has been declining throughout the last decade from 36.1 percent in 2000 to 30.7 percent in 2009 (World Bank 2007, 2011). This is an atypical trend for low-income countries that experience rapid growth periods. Egypt has enjoyed a very prolonged growth phase since the late 1980s, and between 1996 and 2010 the country enjoyed growth rates above 5 percent including peaks of over 7 percent between 2006 and 2008 (www.cbe.org.eg). And the 2009 figure of 30.7 percent is also a very low figure by regional and international standards.

Measurement issues may be a problem of course. Income is not usually well measured, expenditure has often questions of comparability over time, and space and household surveys may not be able to capture all incomes, especially very high and very low incomes. For example, if incomes of the very rich had been growing fast over the past decade and this phenomenon is not captured by the data, real inequality might be much higher than measured inequality and even show a different trend as compared to the one observed with household data. However, measurement problems with household surveys are not unique to Egypt and the question to address in relation to the quality of the household data is whether the quality of the Egyptian data is less good than in other countries, especially in relation to the measurement of welfare among the very poor and the very rich.

We also know from research across the social sciences that the measurement of people's perceptions on any issue is complex. One of the important findings made by scholars across the social sciences in this respect is that perceptions greatly depend on the reference group, the group of people we compare ourselves with. The reference group is mostly composed of people we relate to every day, which means that people captured by the household surveys would compare themselves with other people that are likely to be captured by the same surveys, not with the very top of the population that the surveys may not represent well. According to relative deprivation theories, for example, a middle-income person would make a self-assessment based on peers, usually other middle-income people. If this is true and if the perception of inequality expressed by the street during the revolution had anything to do with income inequality, household surveys would be a good means to observe the relation between facts and perceptions. If, instead, views about inequality are shaped through comparisons with the very rich and the very rich are not captured by household surveys, then it would be natural to observe a mismatch between measured and perceived inequality.

The purpose of this study is to understand whether the observed mismatch between facts and perceptions of inequality in Egypt is a statistical artifact or a true mismatch. The paper looks at the relation between the objective measurement and the subjective judgment of income inequality drawing on three rounds of the Egyptian Household Income, Expenditure and Consumption Survey (HIECS 2000, 2005, 2009) and two rounds of the World Values Surveys (2000 and 2008). It is important to note here that we will focus on the income dimension only. We are interested in the relation between the "facts" about *monetary* inequality and the "perceptions" about *monetary* inequality. The concerns of people in the street obviously span well beyond monetary issues, but in this paper we will focus on the monetary dimension as this is the only dimension for which we have data on both facts and perceptions.

The paper finds that the facts about income inequality and the perceptions about income inequality are both rather accurate. Neither the people nor the data of Egypt are wrong and the mismatch between facts and perceptions effectively holds. The paper also finds numerous leads that could explain such mismatch that can be summarized into one sentence. People judge income inequality based on the distance between their own income expectations and their own realization of these expectations rather than on the distance between their own income and the income of others. If this alternative metric is considered, then facts and perceptions of inequality seem to converge.

The paper is organized as follows. The next section provides a brief overview of what theory and empirics have to say on the possible relation between facts and perceptions of income inequality. The following section is dedicated to addressing issues of measurement of welfare aggregates and comparability of these aggregates over time in an effort to clear most of the concerns that may emerge from the measurement of facts. Next, the paper overviews and compares income and expenditure to see if the two measures convey similar messages. We then estimate inequality and decompose it into its principal components for all the three years considered. The following section turns to the measurement of judgments about income inequality and a final section concludes summarizing the main findings.

Inequality and Inequality Perceptions in Theory and Empirics

Theories on the relation between monetary inequality and the taste for inequality throughout the twentieth century have polarized around two rather extreme views that are nicely represented by the "tunnel effect" theory of Hirschman and Rothschild (1973) and by Runciman's theory of social justice (1966). According to Hirschman and Rothschild (1973): "The tunnel effect operates because advances of others supply information about a more benign external environment; receipt of this information produces gratification; and this gratification overcomes, or at least suspends, envy" (p. 546). (…) "In this eventuality, the increase in income inequality would not only be politically tolerable; it would also be outright desirable from the point of view of social welfare" (p. 548). Although the authors recognize that this effect does not persist in the long term and may be reversed, the tunnel effect theory has provided theoretical support to those believing that income inequality may be beneficial for societies as it provides incentives and rewards for harder-working and more capable people.

Runciman's theory of social justice (1966) later operationalized by Yitzhaki (1979) provides a very different view of the possible relation between inequality and the taste for inequality. According to Runciman, inequality is instrumental in understanding feelings of relative deprivation. Relative deprivation is defined as the feelings of deprivation that accrue to individuals when these individuals compare themselves with a reference group of peers. What matters for feelings of deprivation is not the absolute status but the self-assessment of relative status that derives from comparing one's own situation with the situation of others. In monetary terms, this translates in the fact that an increase in the distance between incomes of peers (an increase in inequality) generates an increase in feelings of deprivation which results in an overall increase in inequality aversion. Yitzhaki (1979) operationalized this idea and proposed to measure relative deprivation as the sum of the distances between one's own income and the incomes of all wealthier individuals and showed how this measure is equivalent to the absolute Gini index. In essence and according to this view, relative deprivation and inequality become one and the same concept and an increase in inequality is expected to lead to an increase in feelings of relative deprivation and inequality aversion.

Understanding the relation between feelings of deprivation and inequality has been historically important for theories of civil strife and revolutions and make this focus particularly important to understand the evolution of perceptions in Egypt during the decade that preceded the 2011 revolution. According to theory, this relation needs to be understood in a broader context where many other factors such as relative status, expectations, or economic conditions may play a role.

Davis (1959), for example, stressed the difference between within-group comparisons and between-group comparisons and how within-group comparisons affect judgments about fairness as opposed to between-group comparisons affecting judgments about subordination. As Runciman (1966), Davis (1959) stresses the importance of the reference group to determine feelings of deprivation but distinguishes between within group and between groups' dynamics. A different perspective is offered by Gurr (1968) who argued in his theory of social strife that people focus on the gap between what they expect to have and what they have, between expectations about possessions and actual possessions. In this context, feelings of deprivation and inequality aversion emerge not in the context of comparisons with other people but in the context of comparisons with one's own expectations. Hence, the search for factors that may explain feelings of deprivation need to pass through the search of factors that affect individual expectations.

Other authors have emphasized instead the role of change in determining feelings of deprivation. Karapetoff (1903) argued: "The degree of life-satisfaction of separate individuals or of whole societies is measured, not by the absolute quantity of goods possessed, but by the rapidity with which this quantity is increasing" (p. 681). Similarly, Davies (1962) in his theory of revolutions stressed that people are more content during periods of growth as opposed to periods of stagnation irrespective of the absolute levels of incomes during the two periods. These views on how people perceive changes in incomes rely on the macroeconomic environment rather than on the comparison with others or the comparison between one's own assets and expectations.

These theories point to a set of key elements that combined together lead to the creation of sentiments about social change. The first element is the construction of the reference group. How people determine their own self-selected reference group which is then used to make assessments of one's own situation. The second element is the relative position of people, where people rank relatively to the reference group. The third element is the mobility of the reference group, how fast peers move up or down in the social scale. The fourth element is the mobility of society overall, the rate of growth of a society. And the fifth element is how—based on the reference group, relative rank, peers mobility, and society mobility—expectations and aspirations are formed and how these expectations and aspiration match the actual conditions of individuals. The combination of these few theories alone leads to a very complex web of relations between facts and perceptions of inequality that are not easily detectable in quantitative research.

This is perhaps part of the reason why empirical results on the relation between facts and perceptions of inequality have been very heterogeneous. The empirical literature is not particularly rich but some important evidence has emerged, especially during the last decade. Morawets et al. (1977) designed an experiment to understand if two communities in Israel differed in average happiness, given the different levels of income inequality and found that the community with less inequality was also the happier one. Alesina, Di Tella, and MacCulloch (2004) found individuals to be less happy where inequality is higher but also found that this relation is much stronger in the European Union (EU) as compared to the United States. Graham and Felton (2006) looking at Latin American countries found inequality to make richer people happier and poorer people unhappier. A study by Clark (2003) finds instead a positive correlation between inequality and happiness among workers, while other studies find no significant correlation between inequality and life satisfaction (Veenhoven, 1996; Senik, 2004). More recently, Verme (2011) has tried to explain such empirical heterogeneity and concluded that the relation between life satisfaction and inequality is generally negative and significant but that issues of multicollinearity can obscure such relation in empirical applications.

While this branch of empirical research is still at an early stage, it provides some preliminary indications on the variables that are relevant to better understand perceptions of changes in incomes and income inequality. For example, it has clearly emerged that is particularly important to look into people's views of politics, institutions, religion, gender, and moral values. In recent years, the increasing availability of values surveys such as the World Values Surveys and the Gallup World Poll have allowed expanding our understanding of people's perceptions of various issues, including perceptions of inequality. Thus, possible clues to our facts-perceptions puzzle may come from the analysis of values surveys, something we will turn to after our analysis of the facts.

Data Quality

Much of the analysis that follows will depend on data quality. This section illustrates the Egyptian consumption data and discusses some of the measurement and comparability issues that could affect a study on inequality.

The study relies on the Household Income, Expenditure and Consumption Survey (HIECS) administered by the Central Agency for Public Mobilization and Statistics (CAPMAS). The survey is conducted approximately every five years and covers a sample of 48,000 households, one of the largest samples among consumption surveys worldwide. However, not all data are provided by CAPMAS to researchers in full. Access was granted to the 2005 sample in full and to 25 percent of the 2000 and 2009 samples extracted randomly, equal to approximately 12,000 households for each year. In terms of variables, this data set provides all the variables that we need for a study on inequality. But in terms of coverage, the random extraction of observations for 2000 and 2009 requires a specific assessment of the implications for measuring inequality.

The sample design of the 1999/2000 survey HIECS is based on the 1996 Population Census. The sample frame includes 600 sampling areas distributed between urban areas (360 units) and rural areas (240 units). The sample is a stratified multistage random sample of 48,000 households and is representative at the national, regional, and governorate level. The master sample is stratified such that urban and rural areas are self-independent strata. Each stratum (urban or rural) is divided into internal layers (governorates). Primary sampling units (PSUs) (areas) were systematically selected, using sampling interval and a random start. Using maps, these areas were further subdivided into a number of chunks of about 1,500 households each with one chunk chosen randomly from each area. Finally, 80 households were selected randomly from each chunk. The sampling errors in the 1999/2000 survey were estimated at 0.7 percent in urban areas and 0.9 percent in rural areas, with 95 percent confidence level.

As described in World Bank (2007): "Two survey forms were used in HIECS, a diary and a main questionnaire. Each household was visited ten times over the course of one month. The enumerator gave the household a diary in the first visit and asked the respondent to report all food expenditures which the household makes every day, for a period of one month. The sum of the daily expenditure was then recorded in the main questionnaire at the end of the interview cycle. Expenditure of non-food items was collected for the previous three months or the previous year depending on the type of commodity. The annualized sum of monthly or quarterly household expenditures was then used to construct the consumption basket for total annual household expenditures. Interviewers took down household demographic information at the first interview and household income at the last two interviews. In brief, consumption is measured as the total sum of food consumption (home produced and markedly purchased), total non-food expenses, and actual or imputed rental value of housing" (Annex 1.1, p. 3, vol. 2).

The 2004/05 survey is a multistage self-weighted area sample of 1,223 PSU of about 700 household each with urban and rural stratification (World Bank 2007). The survey design and sampling is essentially the same used for the previous sample and both samples were constructed on the same 1996 population census frame. The main questionnaire and the diary were also the same. Perhaps the main difference is that data of the 2004/05 survey were collected from July 2004 to June 2005 while data for the previous survey were collected between October 1999 and September 2000. As we consider only annual figures, this should not make any difference for our analysis.

The latest 2008/09 survey contains a number of improvements including a change in the sampling method based on the 2006 population census and a change in the method for collecting food diary data (World Bank 2011). In particular, the change in the sample allowed for reducing the number of households surveyed in each sampling area and the consequent increase in

sampling areas from 1,223 to 2,526. As a result, standard errors for the statistics estimated from the survey decreased and the geographical coverage
improved. The second change was a decision to reduce the food consumption
diary to 15 days instead of 30 days to improve on compliance. The questionnaire was also extended to better measure social transfers and the informal
sector. The quality control procedures were roughly the same as in 2005 but
the quality of these procedures improved. In essence, the 2008/09 survey is
expected to be more accurate and provide better statistics as compared to the
previous two surveys.

Despite the survey improvements described, comparing inequality measures
over time presents a number of challenges. First, welfare aggregates used have
changed over time, especially between 2000 and 2005 and for both income and
expenditure. Second, extracting 25 percent of observations from the original
sample presents estimation difficulties similar (but not equal) to those related to
the sample vis-à-vis the population. Third, the accuracy of estimates has
improved over time and this may affect comparisons over time. Fourth, behavioral patterns in responding to questionnaires may have changed over time, particularly for variables that are more sensitive to this phenomenon such as income.
Fifth, the capacity to capture accurately the two tails of the distribution is typically weak in household surveys, but if this capacity has changed over time, this
may affect the comparison of inequality measures across years.

To address the first issue of comparability of welfare aggregates, we have
reconstructed income and expenditure measures from first components and
reaggregated these measures so as to be comparable over time. This exercise
necessarily implies the use of reduced forms of both income and expenditure
aggregates. In essence, to make these measures comparable we needed to reduce
the measures to the common minimum denominator. For income, this meant to
reduce this measure to four essential components: wages, agricultural income,
nonagricultural income, and transfers. Thus, financial incomes and rents were
excluded because the aggregation of these two items changed over time but also
because the resulting aggregates were found to be very volatile. For expenditure,
we kept 12 items that were identical for the three years. These included: food
and beverages, alcoholic drinks and smokes, clothes, textiles and shoes, residence
and its accessories, furniture, house equipments, health care and services, trans-
portation, telecommunications, culture and entertainment, education, restau-
rants and hotels, and various services and commodities. Therefore, the only
important items excluded from expenditure are transfers, both in kind and in
cash and rents or imputed rents.

The second question concerning the random extraction of 25 percent of
observations is more problematic to address. However, it is possible to test the
relevance of this factor with a simple Monte-Carlo experiment. Using the 2005
sample which is available in full we extracted randomly 100 samples and recalculated each time the Gini index and its standard error. We repeated this exercise
for both income and expenditure and then plotted the resulting Gini indexes
against the respective standard errors. The results are shown in figure 3.1.

Figure 3.1 Random Extraction of 25 Percent Observations (100 Repetitions, 2005 Sample)[a]

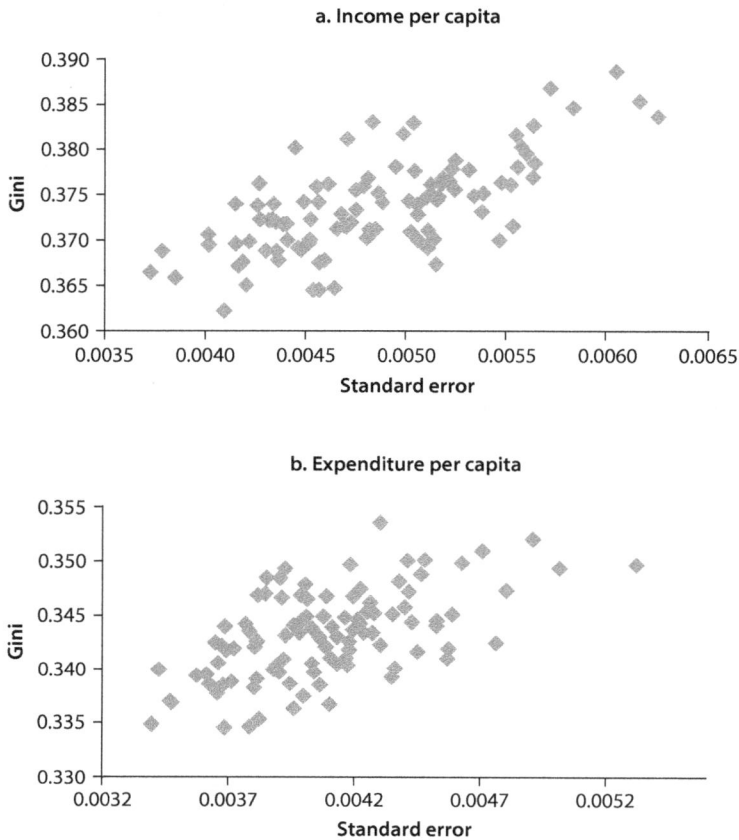

a. Income per capita

b. Expenditure per capita

Source: 2005 HIECS.
a. Note that the inequality analysis in this paper refers to inequality across households. Inequality across individuals is typically lower than inequality across households because income or expenditure is measured at the household level and the per capita figures are equal among household members. Hence, figures of inequality in this paper cannot be compared with figures of other parts of the report or those of other reports that estimate inequality across individuals. HIECS = Household Income, Expenditure and Consumption Survey.

As it can be seen, the Gini for income varies between 36 percent and 39 percent while the Gini for expenditure varies between 33.4 percent and 35.4 percent. These are ranges of three and two percentage points, respectively. The standard errors are not particularly problematic, given the sample size, but we can observe a clear positive correlation between the Gini index and the standard error for both income and expenditure. Confidence intervals (not shown in the graph) for the samples extracted are fairly stable and around 2 percentage points for income and around 1.5 percentage points for expenditure. This means that many of these intervals overlap and that the theoretical range of the Gini estimates extends to the lower bound of the lower estimate and to the upper bound of the upper estimate.

These results provide a rather strong argument for being very cautious when comparing the Gini over time, given that the 2000 and 2009 samples are random extractions from the original samples. Changes in the range of three percentage points for income and two percentage points for expenditure could be fully explained by the random extraction of the 2000 and 2009 samples. The likelihood that the random extraction determines a difference of three or two percentage points is evidently very small (less than 1 percent) but possible while the likelihood of a difference in the range of one percentage point is fairly large and hence very possible.

The third point about the improved accuracy of the surveys cannot be addressed and is not necessarily a drawback for the comparison over time. For the comparison of the 2005 and 2009 survey, we do not expect this issue to be a major constraint. That is because the 2005 sample was available in full while the 2009 sample has improved in accuracy, although we only have a 25 percent sample. These two factors may balance each others' out and are expected to result in good comparability over time. Comparing the 2000 and 2005 surveys is more problematic because the 2005 survey has changed, has improved, and is available in full as opposed to the 2000 survey. Between these two years we really need to be cautious in deriving any definitive conclusion on inequality.

The fourth factor of concern related to changes in behavioral patterns of responses is an issue common to any survey comparison over time, and we do not have elements to suggest that this is a particular feature of our surveys, with one caveat. When we compared data on financial incomes and rents, we found great differences over time and also great volatility of figures. This would suggest that behavioral patterns in responses may have changed over time, but the very fact that we finally excluded these items has addressed the problem and this phenomenon was not observed for the items that we preserved in the income or expenditure aggregates. Therefore, while changes in behavioral response patterns may still exist, we are not expecting this issue to be more pronounced than in consumption surveys elsewhere.

Finally, the fifth question related to the changes in the capacity of the survey to capture the two tails of the distribution can be explored by looking at inequality within quantiles.[1] We calculated the Gini index by ventile for each of the three years considered and plotted the results in figure 3.2. What is immediately evident is that the ventiles with the greatest inequality are found on the two tails of the distributions while the ventiles with the lowest inequality are found in the middle of the distribution. This is not surprising and a feature common to any survey. However, if the survey capacity to capture the two tails of the distribution changes over time, this is bound to have an important effect on the comparison of inequality over time.

In figure 3.2, it is also evident that the curves for the three years overlap throughout the distribution, although this overlap is less evident on the two tails. In fact, a closer look at the top and bottom ventiles indicates that inequality for the bottom 5 percent of households has increased for both income and expenditure throughout the period (table 3.1). By contrast, inequality for the top 5 percent of households has a U-shape, first decreasing between 2000 and 2005 and then increasing between 2005 and 2009, for both income and

Figure 3.2 Gini by Income and Expenditure Ventile

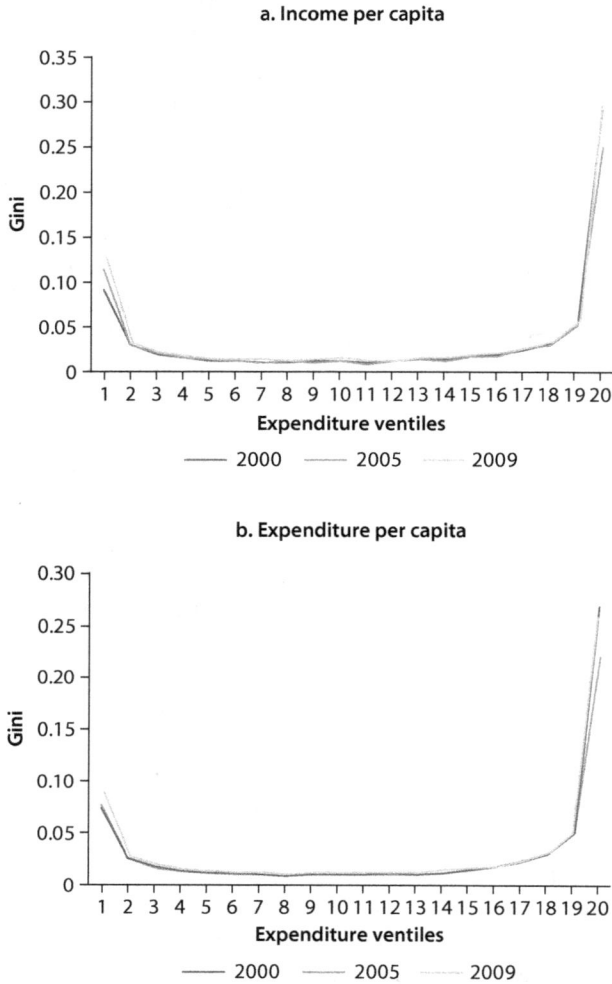

a. Income per capita

b. Expenditure per capita

Source: HIECS 2000, 2005, 2009.
Note: HIECS = Household Income, Expenditure and Consumption Survey.

Table 3.1 Inequality Among the Top and Bottom Ventiles

	2000	*2005*	*2009*
Income per capita			
1st ventile	0.09	0.11	0.12
20th ventile	0.29	0.25	0.30
Expenditure per capita			
1st ventile	0.07	0.08	0.09
20th ventile	0.27	0.22	0.26

Source: HIECS 2000, 2005, 2009.
Note: HIECS = Household Income, Expenditure and Consumption Survey.

expenditure. The fact that the trends for the top and the bottom ventiles are consistent between income and expenditure suggests that these trends are credible. But the fact that the trends on the two tails are different would suggest that these trends cannot be simply explained by an increased or decreased capacity of the survey to capture the two-tail ends of the distribution. If this was the case, both the top and bottom ventiles would be likely to show consistent increasing or decreasing trends, which is not the case. It could be that sampling changes over time have become better in capturing the rich as opposed to the poor or vice versa. But when we discussed sampling design, we saw no element that could support this view. Sampling design progressively improved overall. Changes over time are also rather small on both tails, suggesting that if changes in behavioral responses have occurred, these have not caused major changes in inequality. In essence, this evidence cannot be taken as conclusive but does not point to major problems in relation to changes in behavioral questionnaire responses.

Behavioral consistency over time is of course important for comparability of figures over time but says little about the capacity of the survey to measure inequality in each year well. As discussed above, the main problem in measuring inequality well relates to the two tails of the distribution, the rich in particular. This is a problem of unobserved heterogeneity that we cannot really address in this paper for lack of panel data. We can, however, have a closer look at the relation between top and bottom incomes and at the role that top and bottom incomes play in the measurement of inequality. These two approaches provide some clues on the role of the two tails of the distribution when it comes to measuring inequality.

The relative role of the top and bottom observations can be observed by looking at the top/bottom income and expenditure shares (table 3.2). Here we can see that this share has decreased between 2000 and 2005 and increased between 2005 and 2009 for both income and expenditure. In 2009, the top ventile (5 percent of households), had a mean income more than 17 times higher than the bottom ventile while this figure was 13 times for expenditure. Therefore, the trend over the decade has not been consistent and the difference between 2000 and 2009 is small.

Related to the question of the top/bottom quantile is the question of outliers, which can have an important weight in determining inequality. There is no consensus among scholars on how outliers should be defined or treated but we can comfortably call outliers those observations that represent a very small fraction

Table 3.2 Top-Bottom Ventile Income and Expenditure Share

	2000	2005	2009
Income per capita	16.4	15.8	17.4
Expenditure per capita	13.3	12.1	13.0

Source: HIECS 2000, 2005, and 2009.
Note: HIECS = Household Income, Expenditure and Consumption Survey.

of the sample and that are located on the two extreme ends of the distribution. Here we look at the role of outliers using the 2005 HIECS sample by dividing both income and expenditure into 1,000 quantiles. We then removed the top 10 quantiles and the bottom 10 quantiles one at the time and recalculated each time the Gini. Therefore, we removed 1/1,000 of the sample each time, which is approximately equivalent to removing 48 observations each time. The results are shown in figure 3.3.

Income and expenditure behave almost identically as we have seen before in several of the analyses we conducted, and this is true whether we remove quantiles from the bottom or quantiles from the top. Removing quantiles from the bottom affect the income or the expenditure Gini only marginally, by a fraction of a percentage point for each quantile removal. Instead, removing quantiles from the top has a great effect on the Gini for both income and expenditure. This effect can be of more than 4 percentage points for both income and expenditure when the top ten 1,000ths quantiles (approximately 480 households or 1 percent of total households) are removed.

These findings provide some clues on the importance of the nonobserved top-income households in measuring the real Gini for the population. Suppose, for example, the HIECS did not capture the top 1 percent of households in Egypt. This extra 1 percent is expected to have a distribution with greater variability than the distribution of the last-observed 1 percent of households. Considering

Figure 3.3 Gini Inequality When Removing the Top and Bottom Quantiles (1,000ths)

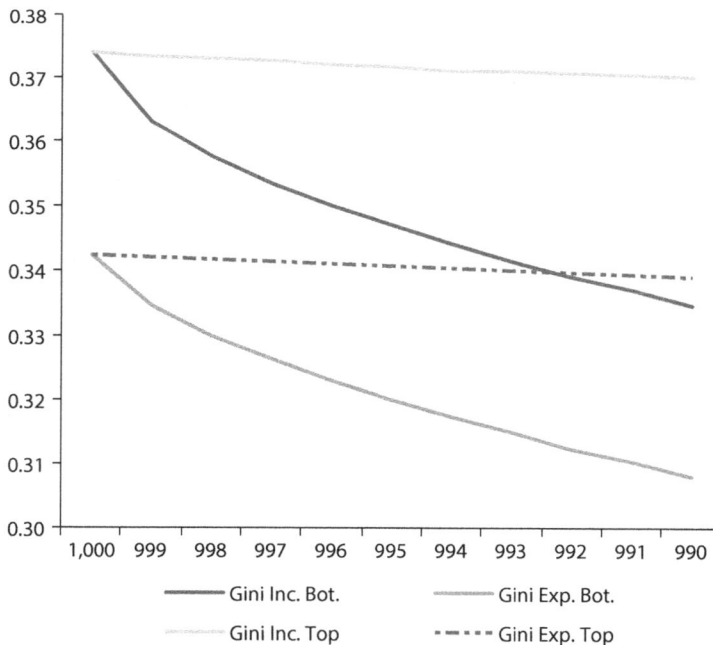

Source: HIECS 2005.

Note: HIECS = Household Income, Expenditure and Consumption Survey.

that the last 1 percent of observed households can affect the Gini by 4 percentage points, this figure should be expected to be a lower bound for the next unobserved 1 percent of households. Moreover, if the households unobserved are more than 1 percent of the sample, this phenomenon becomes greater for each extra 1 percent of unobserved households. We shall conclude therefore that true inequality in Egypt may be much higher than what is actually measured by the HIECS. This is not a unique feature of the HIECS but a common feature of household surveys worldwide. Consumption surveys provide an accurate snapshot of inequality for perhaps 95–97 percent of households but not for all households, especially the very rich who typically refuse to participate to household surveys. This is also an argument for keeping outliers in the analysis when estimating the Gini, because, by removing outliers, we are actually removing the most representative observations of the two tails of the distribution.

One other factor may bias results is missing observations. CAPMAS provided the list of missing observations by primary sampling unit (PSU) for 2009, and this allows us to have a look into this issue. The 2009 sample included 2,526 PSU with an average of 52.4 households each. Of these, 936 PSUs had missing observations, 627 in urban areas (53.5 percent), and 309 in rural areas (22.8 percent). The number of missing observations also varies across PSU. The average share of missing observations for the sample is 3.66 percent, but the average share across PSU with missing observations is 6.99 percent, and this share can vary from 5 percent to 55 percent.

The final data set contains a weight that corrects also for missing observations, but these missing observations may bias our results if, say, richer individuals self-selected themselves out of the sample. It is well known that richer households worldwide tend to self-select themselves out of any sample surveys mostly for lack of interest. As missing observations are not observed by definition, it is very difficult to infer anything about the type of household excluded. What we know is that these households tend to be urban and tend to come from richer governorates but we don't really know if these households are richer or not.

As one tentative experiment, we carried out a cross-PSUs regression by urban and rural areas using as dependent variable the share of missing observations and as independent variables observed income or expenditure (as a measure of household welfare), connections to water and sanitation (as a proxy of local development), and governorates dummies. The idea is that, even if richer households self-selected themselves out of the sample, the remaining observed households could signal richer PSUs, either with average income or expenditure or with better connections to utilities (used here as instruments to signal wealthier PSUs). However, we found no significance among these independent variables (table 3.3). Only when the urban and rural samples were used jointly we found the urban-rural dummy variable to be significant. This would suggest that nonresponses are not related to household welfare but to location, a factor that would not bias estimates on inequality based on welfare measures.

It is also possible that the selection bias was quasi-perfect, meaning that the missing observations make richer PSUs with more missing observations look like

Table 3.3 Explaining Missing Observations by PSUs

| Dep. Var.=% missing | Income | | | Expenditure | | |
obs.	Urban	Rural	Total	Urban	Rural	Total
Income or expenditure	0.0166	0.00878	0.0138	0.0269	0.0191	0.0235
	(0.0349)	(0.0387)	(0.0264)	(0.0361)	(0.0415)	(0.0276)
Water connection	−0.000129	−0.000328	−0.000417	−0.000246	−0.000335	−0.000438
	(0.00359)	(0.00129)	(0.00150)	(0.00359)	(0.00129)	(0.00150)
Sewage connection	0.000537	−0.000302	0.000371	0.000557	−0.000307	0.000376
	(0.00110)	(0.000736)	(0.000669)	(0.00110)	(0.000734)	(0.000668)
Urban areas			−0.229***			−0.227***
			(0.0573)			(0.0573)
Governorates	Yes	Yes	Yes	Yes	Yes	Yes
Constant	2.075***	1.605***	2.381***	1.966***	1.485**	2.269***
	(0.513)	(0.589)	(0.357)	(0.521)	(0.622)	(0.370)

Source: Calculations from missing values data provided by CAPMAS.
Note: CAPMAS = Central Agency for Public Mobilization and Statistics; Dep. Var. = dependent variable; PSU = primary sampling unit.
*** $p<0.01$, ** $p<0.05$, * $p<0.1$.

other PSUs with nonmissing observations. However, the instruments we used of water and sewage connections are never significant in our equations and—within the same PSU—it is unlikely (though possible) that only richer households are connected to these utilities. Therefore, based on this initial analysis, we should conclude that the response rate has more to do with urban-rural location than with welfare.

A recent paper by Hlasny and Verme (2013) confirmed the result that the measurement of income inequality in Egypt using HIECS data is accurate. According to these authors: "This paper utilized a range of recently developed statistical techniques by Korinek et al. (2006, 2007), Cowell and Flachaire (2007), and Atkinson et al. (2011) to assess the true value of income inequality in the presence of a range of possible measurement issues related to top incomes including item and unit non-response, outliers and extreme observations, and atypical top income distributions. The analysis finds that correcting for unit non-response significantly increases the estimate of inequality by just over one percentage point, that the Egyptian distribution of top incomes follows rather closely the Pareto distribution and that the inverted Pareto coefficient is located around median values when compared with 418 household surveys worldwide. Hence, income inequality in Egypt is confirmed to be low while the distribution of top incomes is not atypical as compared to what Pareto had predicted and as compared to other countries in the world" (p. 1).

The Distributions of Income and Expenditure

It is useful at this stage to look at the distributions of our key variables to see whether we can spot any anomaly that could further complicate our study on inequality. Figure 3.4 plots the kernel density distributions for both income and

Figure 3.4 The Distributions of Income and Expenditure Per Capita (2000 Vs. 2009)

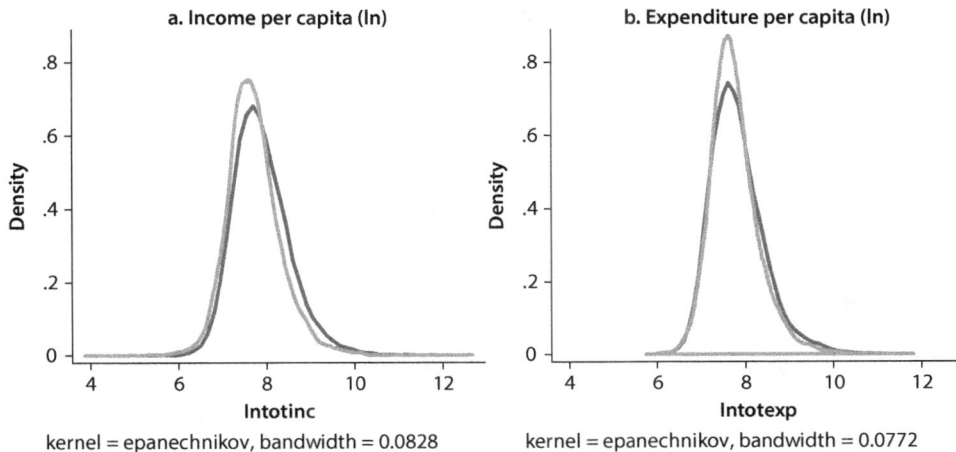

a. Income per capita (ln)

kernel = epanechnikov, bandwidth = 0.0828

b. Expenditure per capita (ln)

kernel = epanechnikov, bandwidth = 0.0772

Source: HIECS 2000, 2009.

expenditure per capita and in real terms (natural logarithm) comparing 2000 with 2009 (the first and last period for which we have 25 percent of the sample). The shapes of the distributions are rather standard for both income and expenditure with a bell-shaped form not particularly skewed in either direction. The distribution of expenditure is more compressed than the income distribution as one would expect, perhaps also because of the reductions we applied to income. Both income and expenditure show that the distributions have shifted leftward over the period indicating a reduction in welfare. This shift took place across the distribution for income while for expenditure the shift seems to have affected mostly the right part of the distribution, where wealthier households are situated.

We can dig further into this analysis by looking at the evolution of income and expenditure by main components as plotted in figure 3.5. If we look at income, we see that income from transfers, wages, and agriculture has first increased between 2000 and 2005 and then declined in 2009. Nonagricultural income has declined throughout the period and so has income per capita overall. These changes are also fairly sharp, especially between 2005 and 2009. Looking at expenditure, we find that food and housing have a bell-shaped development, services a U-shape while clothing shows a declining trend. Overall, expenditure has first increased between 2000 and 2005 and then decreased between 2005 and 2009. In essence, both income and expenditure are consistent in telling a story of declines in the standard of living between 2000 and 2009 with only a marginal improvement visible for expenditure between 2000 and 2005.

To test further the difference between our distributions over time, we can make use of stochastic dominance. Typical stochastic dominance tests imply comparing the Cumulative Distribution Functions—CDFs (first-order stochastic dominance) and the Lorenz curves (second-order stochastic dominance). Figure 3.6 compares the CDFs and the Lorenz curves for the three years

Figure 3.5 Income and Expenditure Components

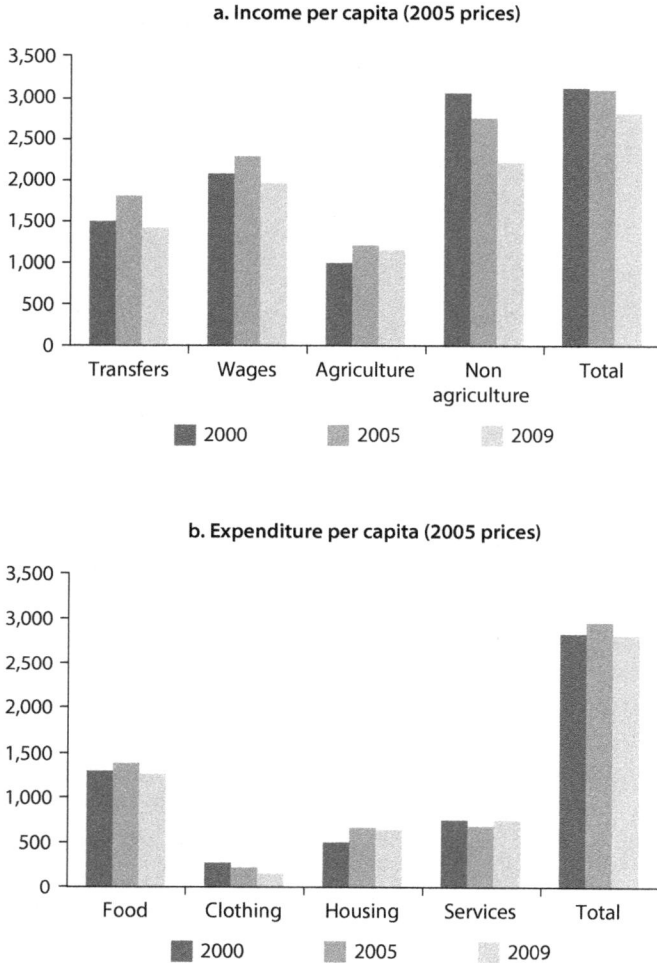

a. Income per capita (2005 prices)

b. Expenditure per capita (2005 prices)

Source: HIECS 2000, 2005, 2009.
Note: Transfers include remittances from abroad.

considered. The curves are fairly close to each other and do not lend themselves to clear-cut interpretations of dominance.

We can, however, test if the curves cross, measure the number of times that these curves cross, and the percentile at which these crossing occur for each pair of years. We can therefore compare 2000–05, 2005–09, and 2000–09 with both income and expenditure per capita. Clearly, the more the two curves intersect, the less clear is dominance of one curve over the other. Also, the more centered are the intersections as opposed to intersections toward the tails of the distributions, the less clear dominance will be.

Table 3.4 provides the results, indicating the number of times that the curves cross, the percentile at which they cross, and the dominance state before each

Figure 3.6 Stochastic Dominance Curves

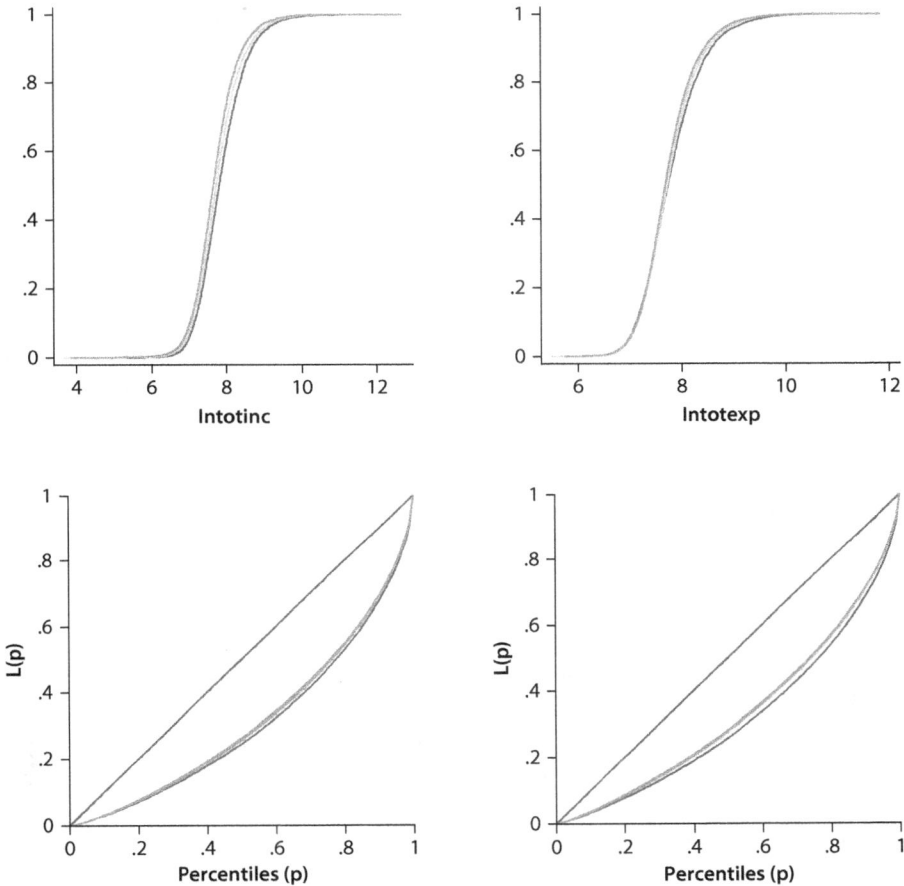

Source: HIECS 2000, 2005, 2009.
Note: HIECS = Household Income, Expenditure and Consumption Survey.

intersection point. All curves for all years intersect at least once. Between 2000 and 2005 we only have one relevant intersection for income around the 36th percentile. In this case, the distribution in the year 2000 lies above that of 2005 until the 36th percentile and below after that. This means that poorer households (below the 36th percentile) did better in 2005 while richer households (above the 36th percentile) did better in 2000. Therefore, income dominance is really a two sides' story during this period.

Between 2005 and 2009, the number of intersections increases for both income and expenditure. However, these intersections occur on the tails of the two distributions so that for the greatest parts of the distributions we can see that 2009 lies above 2005. This means that most households have worsened their situation during the period. Finally, if we compare 2000 and 2009 we only find one relevant intersection for income around the 14th percentile. In this case, the 2000 curve lies above the 2009 curve until the 14th percentile implying that

Table 3.4 Dominance Analysis

(i) Years	(ii) Variable	Intersection	Percentile	Dominance
2000–05	Income	1	0.363	B
		2	0.999	A
2000–05	Expenditure	1	0.039	B
2005–09	Income	1	0	A
		2	0.033	B
		3	0.909	A
		4	0.999	B
2005–09	Expenditure	1	0	A
		2	0.037	B
		3	0.884	A
2000–09	Income	1	0.143	B
		2	0.997	A
		3	0.999	B
2000–09	Expenditure	1	0.038	B
		2	1	A

Source: HIECS 2000, 2005, and 2009.
Note: HIECS = Household Income, Expenditure and Consumption Survey.

poorer households (below the 14th percentile) did better in 2009 than in 2000 but also that most of the distribution between the 14th and the 99th percentile did worse. In essence, these data confirm that the overall situation of households has worsened during the decade but they also revealed that this worsening has mainly affected the middle and upper class while the poorest households have done, on average, better.

For the question of perceptions that will be discussed later, it is also useful to know what is the proportion of households that actually experienced low-income spells, at least on one occasion during the decade. Marotta et al. (2011) used a panel subcomponent of the HIECS to look at labor mobility between 2005 and 2009 and find similar results to ours in terms of the evolution of expenditure over the period. They also find that, when using dynamic poverty profiles, less than 50 percent of households have been consistently out of poverty between 2005 and 2009. Therefore, even if the poverty rate hovered around 20 percent during the period (World Bank 2007, 2011), the number of people who have experienced a poverty spell is much greater, and this is likely to have an impact on the perception of welfare, including the perception of inequality.

What is rather remarkable of the analysis conducted thus far is how similar are income and expenditure and how they convey consistently similar stories. This is rather unusual in low- and low-middle-income countries. For example, in low-income countries, income tends to be largely underestimated to an extent that mean income is typically found to be below mean expenditure. Moreover, the distribution of income is also typically rather different in shape to the distribution of expenditure with different skews of the two curves. In Egypt and despite the restricted definitions used, we find mean income to be higher than mean expenditure in all years and we also find the two curves to be rather similar in shape. Thus, findings consistent between income and expenditure—as we found so far—validate each other and also give us some confidence in the use of these data for the inequality analysis that follows.

Inequality in Income and Expenditure

This section turns to measuring inequality in income and expenditure over time and across households based on the same income and expenditure measures already discussed. Table 3.5 shows the evolution of the Gini coefficient between 2000 and 2009. According to both income and expenditure figures, the Gini has declined, from 37.8 percent to 36.6 percent for income and from 36 percent to 33.8 percent for expenditure. The upper and lower bounds of all figures over the three years considered overlap suggesting that the decline in inequality is not robust. Considering also that the random extraction of the 2000 and 2009 samples can explain up to 3 percent of changes in income and up to 2 percent of changes in expenditure, these figures cannot be taken as a definitive statement on the evolution of inequality.

However, a number of considerations would suggest that these figures are credible and that they show a nonincreasing trend. First, both income and expenditure concord in the trend, telling once more the same story. Second, the 3 percent margin for income is an extreme case with very low likelihood of occurrence. The decline of 1.2 percent in inequality observed for income is not necessarily explained by the random extraction of the 2000 and 2009 samples, and even if that was the case, we cannot conclude that inequality has increased. Also, the margins that random extraction can explain for expenditure are in the maximum range of 2 percent, whereas the decline in expenditure between 2000 and 2009 was of 2.2 percent. Therefore, we can safely conclude that expenditure inequality has declined in Egypt between 2000 and 2009, although the size of the decline may be smaller (or bigger) of what we measured. Overall and considering both income and expenditure, while we cannot conclude with certainty

Table 3.5 Gini Index 2000–09

	Gini	Std.err.	Lower bound	Upper bound
Income per capita				
2000	0.378	0.005	0.368	0.388
2005	0.374	0.002	0.369	0.379
2009	0.366	0.008	0.350	0.382
Expenditure per capita				
2000	0.360	0.004	0.351	0.368
2005	0.342	0.002	0.338	0.346
2009	0.338	0.005	0.328	0.348

Source: HIECS 2000, 2005, 2009.
Note: HIECS = Household Income, Expenditure and Consumption Survey; Std. Err = Standard error.

that inequality has declined, we can safely argue that inequality has not increased between 2000 and 2009.

The Gini index is one of the many inequality indexes that can be estimated, and it is known that the Gini index tends to attribute more weight to the central observations of the distribution and less weight to the tails of the distribution, which we saw being important for measuring inequality. As a test of how robust are the trends in inequality observed with the Gini index, we also measure expenditure inequality using various other inequality measures including the Atkinson index, the General Entropy measures (with alfa=1 and alfa=0.5), the coefficient of variation, and the top/bottom deciles share. Results are shown in table 3.6.

All inequality indexes with no exception show declines in inequality between 2000 and 2009. There is some discordance on the trend between 2005 and 2009 with two indexes showing a decline in inequality, two indexes showing an increase and one index showing no change. The lower and upper bounds for this last period also largely overlap for all indexes and there are not definitive conclusions about the period 2005–09. However, these indexes confirm that inequality has not increased between 2000 and 2009. If anything, the Gini index underestimates the decline in inequality as compared with other inequality indexes.

Table 3.6 Inequality Indexes Compared 2000–09 (Expenditure)

	Value	Std.err.	Lower bound	Upper bound
Atkinson				
2000	0.121	0.004	0.113	0.128
2005	0.098	0.001	0.096	0.101
2009	0.098	0.004	0.091	0.106
General entropy (alfa=1)				
2000	0.292	0.013	0.266	0.317
2005	0.230	0.005	0.221	0.239
2009	0.235	0.014	0.208	0.262
General entropy (alfa=0.5)				
2000	0.249	0.008	0.233	0.265
2005	0.202	0.003	0.196	0.208
2009	0.201	0.008	0.185	0.217
Coefficient of variation				
2000	1.084	0.061	0.964	1.204
2005	0.889	0.026	0.838	0.939
2009	0.980	0.098	0.789	1.172
Top/bottom deciles				
2000	4.36	0.06	4.24	4.47
2005	3.93	0.03	3.88	3.99
2009	3.73	0.05	3.63	3.83

Source: HIECS 2000, 2005, 2009.
Note: HIECS = Household Income, Expenditure and Consumption Survey; Std. Err = standard error.

Table 3.7 Gini by Income and Expenditure Component

	2000	*2005*	*2009*
Income per capita			
Transfers	0.56	0.58	0.61
Wages	0.41	0.41	0.40
Agriculture	0.51	0.53	0.53
Non agriculture	0.54	0.48	0.49
Expenditure per capita			
Food	0.28	0.28	0.27
Clothing	0.43	0.41	0.37
Housing	0.43	0.43	0.45
Services	0.58	0.55	0.52

Source: HIECS 2000, 2005, 2009.
Note: HIECS = Household Income, Expenditure and Consumption Survey.

Exploring inequality by income and expenditure component provides some additional insights into the evolution of inequality. As shown in table 3.7, inequality within components is higher than overall inequality. For income, this is explained by the fact that not all households receive all forms of incomes, given that some households will be prevalently made of employees with wages while others will be prevalently made of self-employed people. When we consider all forms of income at the national level, these differences tend to cancel each other out but within component there may be great differences across households. Also for expenditure, inequality within components tends to be higher than the total aggregates, although this phenomenon is less visible than for income.

For income, transfers is the component with the highest inequality. This component includes interhouseholds transfers as well as government transfers. The largest contributors to this component are interhousehold in-kind and in-cash transfers, which suggests that these transfers play an important role for income inequality. For expenditure, services is the component that shows the highest inequality. As one would expect, as we move away from essential goods and toward less essential goods (from food to clothing, to housing, and to services), inequality tends to increase.

If we consider these components over time, we also see that not all components behave as the national aggregates, which we saw declining (or not increasing) over the period 2000–09. For example, the Gini for transfers and agricultural income have increased during the period as opposed to the Gini for wages and nonagricultural income. For expenditure, all items have decreased in line with the national figures with the exception of housing that has increased, suggesting that the trends in expenditure are not necessarily related to necessities. Inequality among expenditure on services, for example, has decreased even more than inequality on food expenditure.

As we have already observed, inequality is not homogeneous across quantiles when we noticed that the bottom and top ventiles exhibited the greatest

Figure 3.7 Lorenz Curves by Quintiles

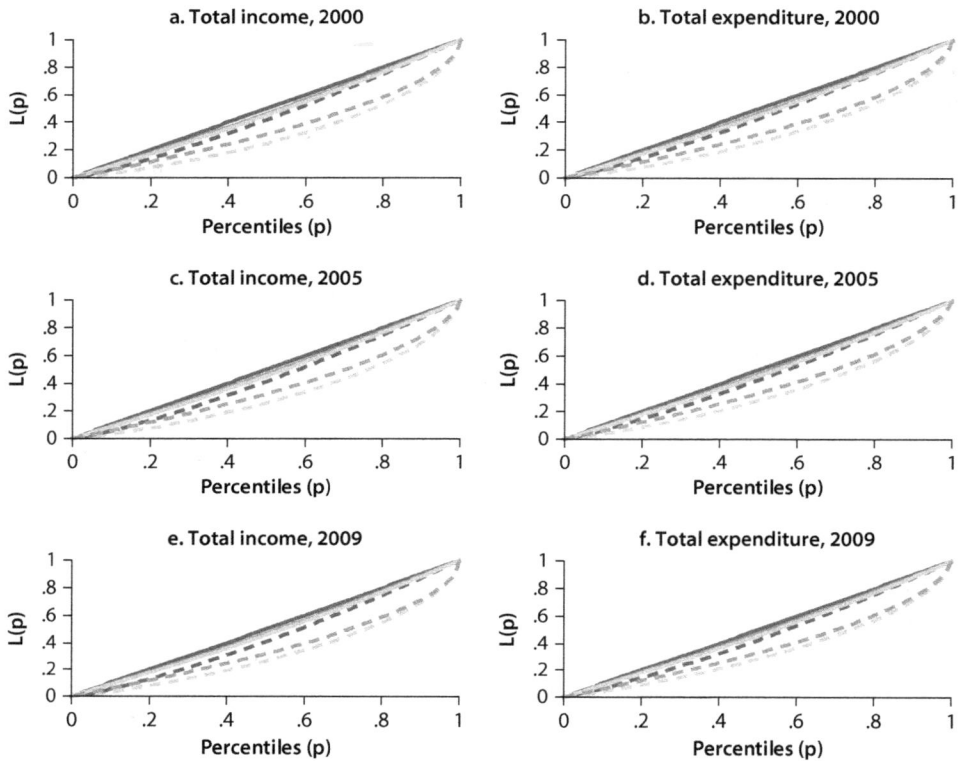

Source: HIECS 2000, 2005, 2009.
Note: HIECS = Household Income, Expenditure and Consumption Survey; totinc = total income; totexp = total expenditure.

within-quantile inequality. This can be also appreciated by looking at the Lorenz curves by quintiles for the different years and for income and expenditure. Figure 3.7 shows the results. The top two quintiles are those that clearly show the highest levels of inequality for both income and expenditure, whereas the first three quintiles tend to overlap. This would speak of a two-tier society with great homogeneity in lower parts of the distributions but also great nonhomogeneity in higher parts of the distributions.

Drivers of Inequality

As it is now standard in welfare analyses, the Gini index can be decomposed in its main components, for both income and expenditure (table 3.8). As far as income is concerned, in 2000 wages were the biggest component and also the most important contributor to inequality explaining 38 percent of total income inequality. This is followed closely by nonagricultural income (37 percent) and transfers (25 percent) while agricultural income does not seem to

Table 3.8 Gini Decomposition, by Component (Income and Expenditure)

		Income share	Relative contribution		Expenditure share	Relative contribution
2000	Transfers	0.22	0.25	Food	0.46	0.33
	Wages	0.42	0.38	Clothing	0.10	0.10
	Agriculture	0.13	0.00	Housing	0.18	0.18
	Nonagriculture	0.24	0.37	Services	0.27	0.40
	Total	**1.00**	**1.00**	**Total**	**1.00**	**1.00**
2005	Transfers	0.21	0.28	Food	0.47	0.35
	Wages	0.46	0.42	Clothing	0.08	0.07
	Agriculture	0.14	0.05	Housing	0.22	0.24
	Nonagriculture	0.19	0.25	Services	0.23	0.34
	Total	**1.00**	**1.00**	**Total**	**1.00**	**1.00**
2009	Transfers	0.23	0.30	Food	0.45	0.32
	Wages	0.45	0.39	Clothing	0.05	0.04
	Agriculture	0.14	0.07	Housing	0.23	0.27
	Nonagriculture	0.18	0.24	Services	0.27	0.37
	Total	**1.00**	**1.00**	**Total**	**1.00**	**1.00**

Source: HIECS 2000, 2005, 2009.
Note: HIECS= Household Income, Expenditure and Consumption Survey.

have any role in explaining inequality. This ranking changes in 2005 and 2009 with transfers becoming the second most important factor after wages while agricultural income continues to play a negligible role.[2] Agricultural income may be expected to be subject to sharp fluctuations over seasons and over the years but it is clearly rather equal across households, most of which are expected to be rural households. This is not an atypical finding in both poor and rich countries. More interesting is perhaps the fact that transfers change position in rank in 2005 and 2009 becoming more important than nonagricultural incomes. That is because most transfers are public transfers, which should be expected to be fairly stable over time and have egalitarian rather than nonegalitarian effects.

Considering expenditure, in 2000 food was the most important component share but the most important contributor to inequality was services explaining alone 40 percent of inequality despite representing only 27 percent of expenditure. Food comes into second place with 33 percent of total inequality explained. Housing and clothing follow in this order. In 2005, the ranking between food and services in explaining inequality is reversed with food now explaining 35 percent of inequality as compared to 34 percent for services. In 2009, the original ranking is restored with services being the highest contributor to inequality with 37 percent of total inequality explained. Given the diversity in the types of services considered, it is not surprising that services explain the greatest share of inequality. This makes the 2005 ranking where food comes on top the most surprising finding on expenditure. Perhaps the sharp fluctuations in food prices that characterized the period worldwide may partly explain this phenomenon.

Summarizing our results on inequality measurement, we can conclude that the HIECS is a good and consistent instrument to measure inequality of observed households. Both income and expenditure tell consistently the same story about inequality, and the finding that inequality has not increased between 2000 and 2009 is robust despite all the caveats that we discussed about the measurement of inequality.

Micro Data Vs. Macro Data

Before we turn to the perceptions of income inequality in Egypt, it is instructive to compare the evolution of gross domestic product (GDP) per capita measured from the national accounts to the evolution of household income per capita measured by the HIECS (figure 3.8). It is often assumed that if GDP per capita in a given country is growing, then households are consequently enjoying better standards of living. This is not always the case as described below for Egypt, and

Figure 3.8 GDP, HH Income and Expenditure (Per Capita, Real Terms, 2000=100)

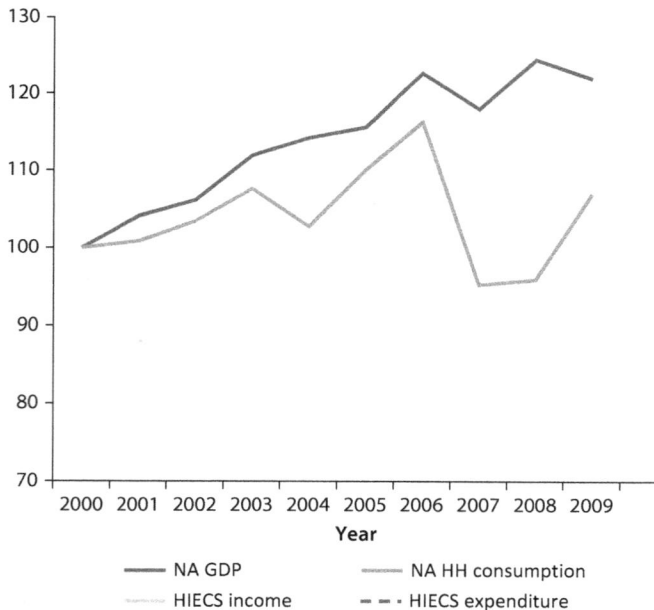

Source: HIECS 2000, 2005, 2009, CAPMAS National Accounts and IMF Economic Outlook database. All data deflated with the IMF CPI inflation rate.[a]
Note: CAPMAS = Central Agency for Public Mobilization and Statistics; CPI = consumer price index; GDP = gross domestic product; HH = household head; HIECS = Household Income, Expenditure and Consumption Survey; IMF = International Monetary Fund; NA GDP = National Accounts gross domestic product. NA HH = National Accounts household head.
a. Trends in HIECS data are not entirely comparable with previous sections due to the use of a different deflator.

this particular mismatch between GDP growth and household income growth can be one of the pieces explaining the mismatch between facts and perceptions of inequality.

Between 2000 and 2009 and according to national accounts, GDP per capita has grown by about 22 percent in cumulated terms while household consumption has grown by about 8 percent. Thus, national accounts show that household consumption has not kept up with GDP growth over the decade. Moreover, according to the HIECS survey data, household income has declined by about 15 percent while household consumption has declined by about 8 percent. Therefore, we can estimate a gap of 37 percent for income and 16 percent for consumption between the macro data and the micro data. Such mismatch witnesses that GDP growth has not trickled down to households, a fact that cannot have gone unnoticed to households.

But where has all the GDP growth gone? Figure 3.9 plots GDP per capita growth at market prices and by component according to the national accounts classification. It is evident that financial institutions (banks) experienced a negative growth while household consumption stagnated as discussed above. The real winners during the period are nonfinancial institutions (private enterprises), nongovernment organizations, and government in this order with the

Figure 3.9 Sources of GDP Per Capita Growth (2000 Market Prices)

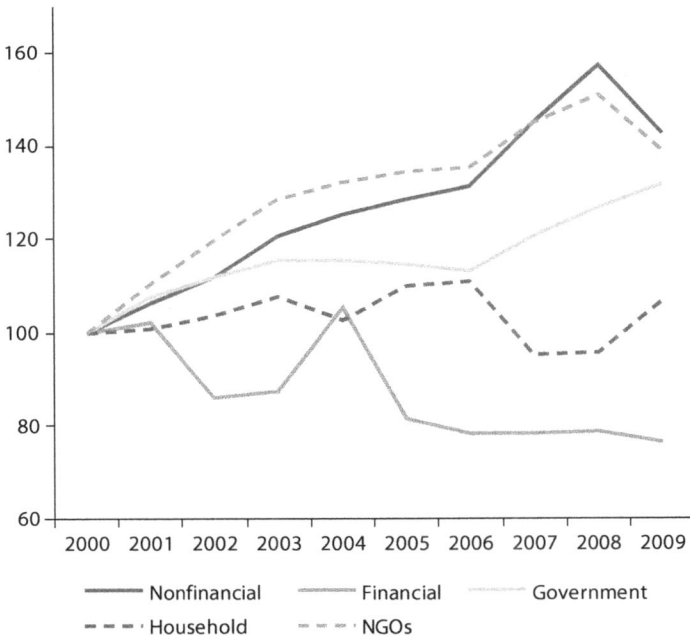

Sources: CAPMAS National Accounts and IMF Economic Outlook database.
Note: CAPMAS = Central Agency for Public Mobilization and Statistics; GDP = gross domestic product; IMF = International Monetary Fund; NGOs = nongovernmental organizations.

first two sectors growing by over 40 percent in cumulated terms over the period. Private enterprises in particular seem to have retained earnings or having transferred earnings abroad rather than distributing earnings via wages and dividends or investing domestically. Therefore, while households may well have observed wealth growing in the public and private sectors, they have seen little accruing to their own pockets. This has surely had an effect on sentiments of deprivation and on the perception of inequality, the question to which we turn to now.

Perceptions of Inequality and Its Correlates

In this section, we turn to explore changes in perceptions of income inequality of the Egyptian population during the last decade. For this purpose, we use two rounds of the World Values Surveys (WVSs) which have been administered in Egypt in 2000 and 2008, two years that almost coincide with the first and the last HIECS surveys we used in previous sections.[3] Given the different nature and contents of the HIECSs and WVSs, these data sets cannot be merged so that we cannot study the relation between the HIECSs' income and expenditure and the WVSs perceptions of welfare. However, the WVSs contain questions on income and social classes and perceptions of inequality which can be studied in conjunction.

The WVSs are perhaps the most established and long-running world surveys on values, perceptions, and opinions usually covering in between 1,500 and 4,000 observations per country.[4] The Egyptian samples are among the largest samples including 3,000 observations for 2000 and 3,051 for 2008. The WVSs are typically long questionnaires. Over 900 variables have been constructed to date starting from these questionnaires, although not all questions are administered in all countries and in all years. The set of variables that have been constructed for Egypt and that are common to the years 2000 and 2008 include 140 variables covering themes such as family values, trust, gender, politics, religion, expectations about the future, and a number of personal characteristics such as age, gender, and education. The surveys also include questions on happiness, life satisfaction, satisfaction with the financial situation of the household, social status, and income classes. One question asks respondents about their subjective perceptions of inequality. We can therefore relate this question with all other variables present in the survey and learn about the changing nature of the perception of inequality over the decade that preceded the 2011 revolution.

As discussed at the outset of the paper, one of the factors that may drive perceptions about inequality relate to macroeconomic changes and the speed of these changes. During the decade 2000–10, some of the key macroeconomic indicators for Egypt looked rather good and were also changing fairly fast. We should also keep in mind that the decade considered has been characterized by high-price volatility and the 2007–08 global crisis. While these factors may not have affected the Egyptian economy to a great degree, they might have affected people's perceptions of the economy. High-price instability and the global crisis may have increased fears about the future, even for those households that may have done better overall.

Indeed, this period of macroeconomic growth and price instability has changed people's expectations and priorities. The WVSs contain questions on priorities for individuals and the government, some of which we plotted in figure 3.10. According to respondents, economic growth has risen very significantly among the factors that people think should be a government priority (top panel). This greater emphasis on economic growth has happened at the expens-

Figure 3.10 People's Shifting Priorities 2000–08

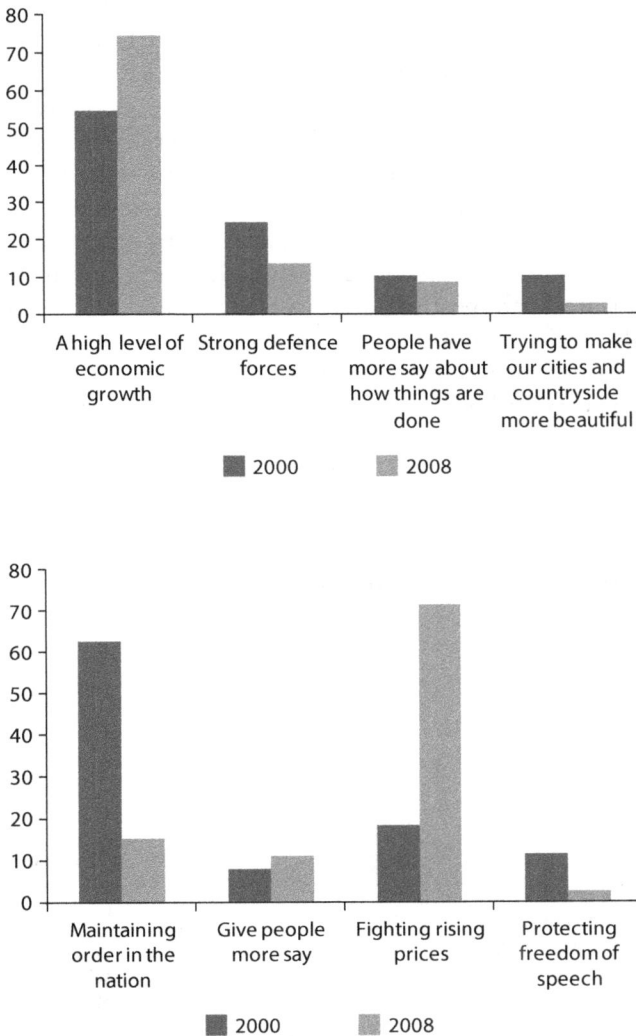

Source: WVSs 2000 and 2008.
Note: WVS = World Values Surveys.

es of views about defense, people's voice, and environmental concerns. Price volatility during the last decade has also played an important role in changing people's priorities (right panel). Fighting rising prices became by far the most important priority as compared to maintaining order, give people more say, or protecting freedom of speech. In essence, during a decade of growth and price instability, these two themes became top priorities in people's minds as opposed to factors such as people's voice and freedom of speech, two aspects that have been closely associated with the Egyptian revolution.[5]

In the backdrop of such changes in the economics and people's priorities, were Egyptians in 2008 happier than in 2000? Revolutions are evidently driven by discontent and we may want to see if a rise in discontent is visible between 2000 and 2008. In figure 3.11, we compare the density functions of 2000 (in blue) and 2008 (in red) for replies to a question on life satisfaction and satisfaction with the financial situation of the household (both questions on a 1–10 scale with "1" indicating very low satisfaction and "10" indicating very high satisfaction).

Remarkably, the density distributions of answers to these questions have changed very significantly over the period for both life satisfaction and the household financial satisfaction. In both cases, the distributions shifted from a dual mode distribution to a more hump-shaped distribution. It is as if in 2000 the society was completely polarized around happy and unhappy people, whereas in 2008 the distributions became much more smooth and typical of such categorical ordered variables with most respondents being around the center of the ladder. Interestingly, while mean life satisfaction has slightly increased from 5.3 to 5.7, mean financial satisfaction has declined from 5.2 to 4.8, showing that life satisfaction is not solely guided by financial satisfaction. Yet, it is not so much the mean change in satisfaction that is remarkable here but the change in the shape of the distributions. These findings could be interpreted as people shifting from a more extreme and fatalistic view of life to a more conscious and accurate

Figure 3.11 Life and Financial Satisfaction, 2000 (Blue) and 2008 (Red)

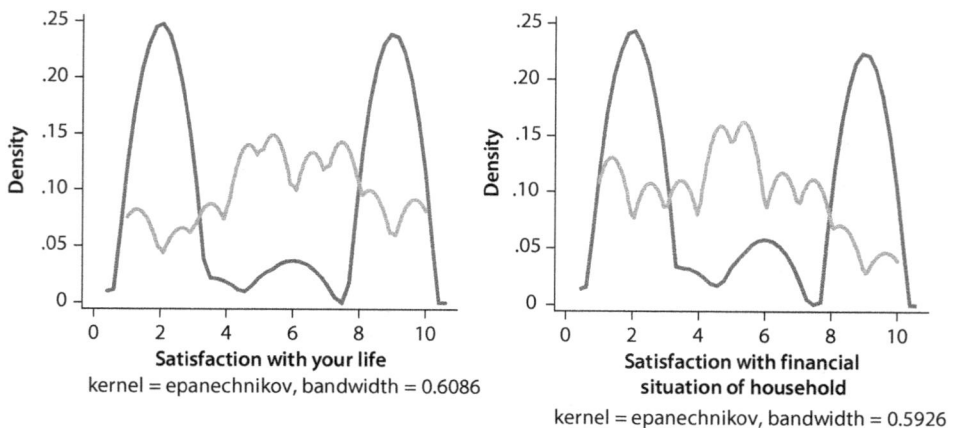

kernel = epanechnikov, bandwidth = 0.6086

kernel = epanechnikov, bandwidth = 0.5926

Source: WVSs 2000 and 2008.
Note: WVS = World Values Surveys.

view of one's proper situation. Whatever the explanation, the changes observed in the distribution of answers are remarkable.

Perceptions on welfare have also changed during the decade. In the previous sections, we found that the welfare situation of households has worsened marginally over the decade 2000–09, even if this trend has not affected all households in the same manner, with poorer households doing better than richer households. Above, we also saw that the average satisfaction with the financial situation of the household has declined. With the WVSs, we can see further whether Egyptians have actually perceived changes in welfare across income and social classes.

Figure 3.12 depicts the density curves of replies to a question on income and a question on social class. Respondents were asked to tell to what level of the

Figure 3.12 Changes in Income and Social Class Perceptions

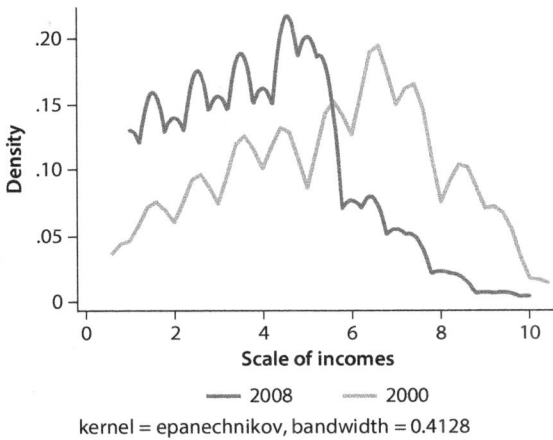

kernel = epanechnikov, bandwidth = 0.4128

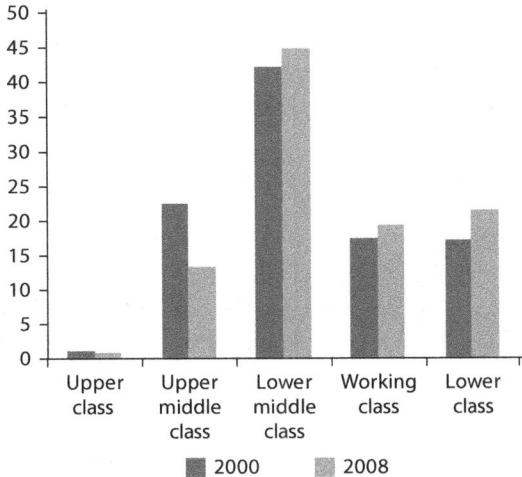

Source: WVSs 2000, 2008.
Note: WVS = World Values Survey.

Inside Inequality in the Arab Republic of Egypt • http://dx.doi.org/10.1596/978-1-4648-0198-3

income scale they belonged to on a scale from 1 to 10 and they were also asked to declare to what social class they belonged to among five different social classes. While the income class question was structured by income brackets in local currency and is therefore a more objective way of measuring self-declared income, the social class question is largely subjective. By comparing the density curves for 2000 and 2008, we can clearly see how self-declared welfare status has changed.

Egyptians reported to be much poorer in 2008 as compared to 2000. The share of respondents reporting to belong to the top four steps (the richest) of the income ladder (top panel) has clearly dropped in favor of those who reported to be on lower-income steps (bottom panel). It can be clearly seen that the two curves cross around the sixth decile witnessing unequivocally the change in perceptions. The same trend can be observed by looking at changes in perceptions about social classes (bottom panel). Here we see that the share of respondents who argued to belong to the top two classes (upper class and upper-middle class) has clearly declined in favor of lower social classes. Therefore, Egyptians have felt the downgrade in welfare documented with the HIECS data. Published positive macroeconomic figures on GDP did not do much to change perceptions of the average Egyptian. In fact, welfare perceptions seem to have declined even more than welfare itself.

Income and social classes are not equivalent or equidistant concepts or concepts that express the same rank. This is also visible by comparing people's answers to these questions (figure 3.13). When people place themselves on the social class scale, they do so with a bias toward upper social classes, while when they place themselves on the income scale, they place themselves on relatively lower-income classes.[6] This phenomenon existed but was not very visible in 2000 when big differences existed mainly for the lower-income and social class. Instead in 2008, both the social and income class ranking moved downward with the income ranking moving downward faster. It is rather natural for social classes to be less mobile than income classes as people may change income more frequently than they change occupation, residence, or peers, which help in defining social class. But again, what is important to remark here, it is the change in views between 2000 and 2008 and the relative fall in income and social status.

We may also want to compare answers to the question on income classes in the WVSs to the distribution of incomes in the HIECS. These two variables are not really comparable in any particular year. That is because the samples and questions in the two surveys are different, the HIECS measure is household income per capita while the WVS measure is income of the respondent and the answers to the WVS question is also influenced by subjective perceptions of incomes. However, it is interesting to compare changes over time in the relation between the HIECS and WVS monetary indicators. This can be done by constructing from the HIECS frequencies distributions using the same income classes used for the WVS question. We also tried to adjust total household income in the HIECS by the number of dependents rather than per capita so as

Figure 3.13 Social Classes Vs. Income Classes, 2009

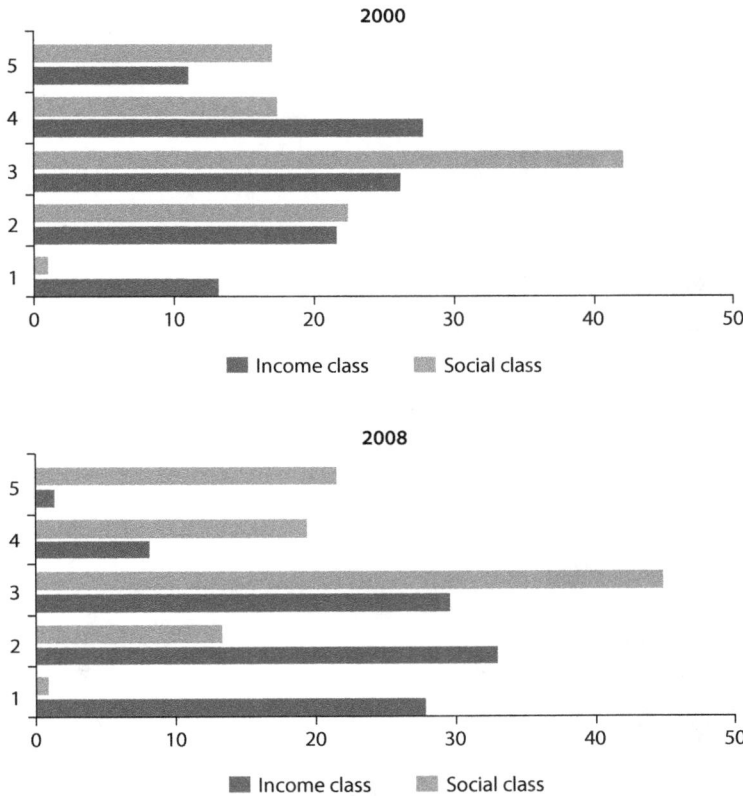

2000

2008

Source: WVS 2000, 2008.
Note: WVS = World Values Survey.

to make it closer to the WVS income measure that captures only individual adults. Results are shown in figure 3.14.

The HIECS and WVS distributions are remarkably close in 2000 with the exception of the 5th, 8th and 9th deciles. Between 2000 and 2008/09, both distributions shift leftwards conveying the same story that welfare in real terms has decreased over the period. However, the leftward shift of the WVS distribution is much more pronounced than that of the HIECS so that the 2009 HIECS and WVS distributions become clearly different. Given that the WVS distribution is also affected by subjective factors, this could be interpreted as Egyptians becoming more pessimistic about their own income situation relatively to changes in their own actual situation. It is as if the mismatch between welfare and welfare expectations has increased between 2000 and 2008.

Given the increased disillusionment about their own income and status situation, have Egyptians changed their own perception of inequality? The WVSs do not ask direct questions on the level of inequality but ask respondents whether they have a preference for more or less inequality. The question is phrased as

Figure 3.14 HIECS Vs. WVS Income Distributions

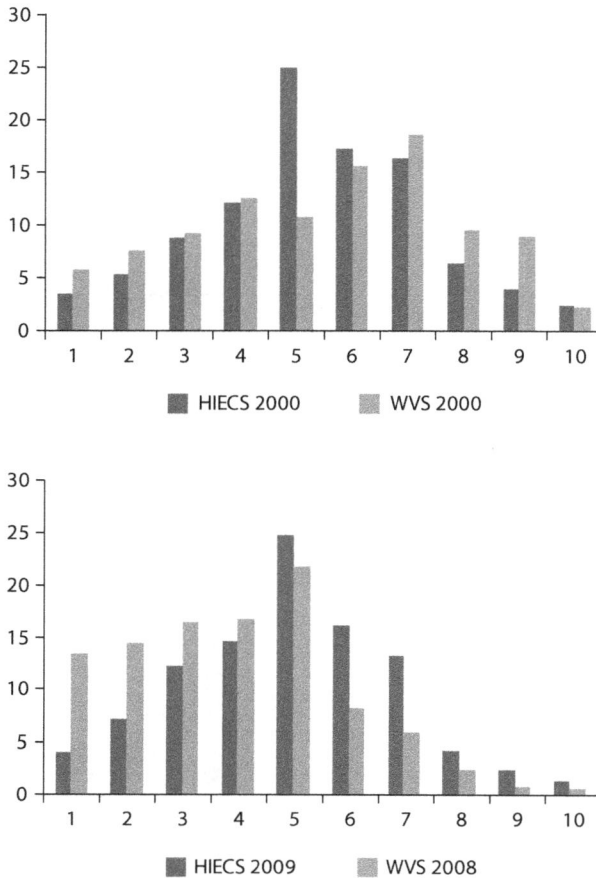

HIECS 2000   WVS 2000

HIECS 2009   WVS 2008

Source: HIECS 2000, 2009 and WVS 2000, 2008.
Note: HIECS = Household Income, Expenditure and Consumption Survey; WVS = World Values Survey.

follows: *How would you place your views on this scale? "1" means you agree completely with the statement on the left (Incomes should be made more equal); "10" means you agree completely with the statement on the right (We need larger income differences as incentives).* In previous sections, we learned that income inequality has not increased over the decade. Here we see how Egyptians have changed attitudes towards income inequality.

Figure 3.15 (top panel) depicts the results by plotting the density curves of the replies for the two years considered. What we see is a clear shift towards inequality aversion. In particular, the share of those who were greatly in favor of higher income differences as incentives dropped substantially in favor of more moderate views or in favor of the view that incomes should be made more equal. The curves for the two years intersect around the 7th and 8th steps, leaving little doubts about the fact that perceptions about inequality have shifted leftwards. Despite non increases in inequality, Egyptians clearly turned towards inequality aversion.

Figure 3.15 Taste for Inequality by Income Groups

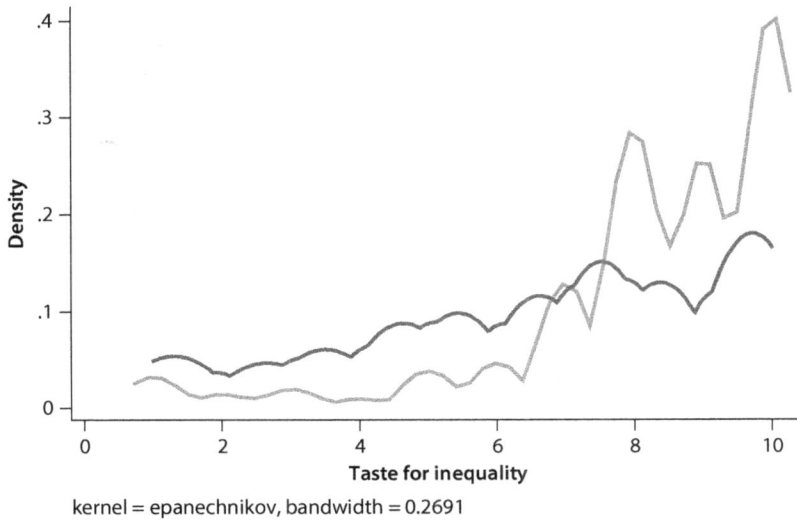

kernel = epanechnikov, bandwidth = 0.2691

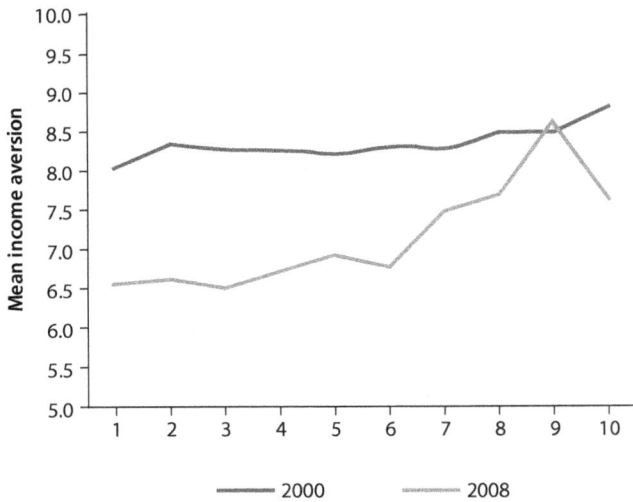

Source: WVS 2000, 2008.
Note: WVS = World Values Survey.

Given that the poor seem to have done better than the rich during the period considered, it is worth to see now whether different income classes have a different appreciation of inequality. Some of the theory and empirical literature that we reviewed at the beginning of this paper argued that different income classes have a different appreciation of inequality. In figure 3.15 (bottom panel), we plotted mean inequality aversion per each income group as defined by the self-assigned income class question. The taste for inequality has been declining sharply for almost all income groups but not for all. The taste for inequality is generally higher for higher income groups as one would expect but the difference across groups is rather small in 2000. In 2008, with the general increase in inequality aversion, the difference across income groups becomes much larger with richer income groups showing a much higher appreciation of inequality as compared to the poorest groups.

In the context of the different performance of the different income groups, this finding lends itself to a particular interpretation. The middle and upper class that seems to have lost more from the welfare analysis we conducted before reduced its pro-inequality stand but less than the poor, or even increased as it is shown for the 9th decile. The lower deciles who have done a bit better during the decade show instead a greater drop in the appreciation of inequality. It is as if the lower deciles (who have done relatively better) came to better understand their relative status and grew their dislike for such status by voting against inequality. We may see here the role of changing reference groups. Lower deciles might have acquired a better sense of their position in society and by gaining ground on upper deciles they might be comparing themselves more and more with richer people and, by doing so, they might better appreciate the injustice related to their relative position. This is of course one of the possible interpretations but one that is consistent with the findings on satisfaction where we argued that the shift from a dual mode distribution to a more normal distribution might be explained by a shift from a more fatalistic view of life to a more conscious and pragmatic view of people's own relative status.

We can further test the association between income and social class and the taste for inequality by means of standard econometrics. In table 3.9 we report the results of an ordinary least squares (OLS) regression using taste for inequality as dependent variable and income classes and social classes as independent variables separately. We run the regression for both 2000 and 2008 controlling for a number of variables including gender, age, marital status, education, employment status, location (town size larger or smaller than 50,000 people and region), and savings[7] By controlling for individual characteristics we control for possible changes in population structure between the two surveys, given the small size of the samples. The variable savings was added to indicate whether the household has managed to save during the past 12 months and is meant to control for the recent performance of the household as opposed to income and social status which are more permanent conditions.

Results reveal several insights into the relation between income and social status and the taste for inequality. The first observation is that income or social status (together with the controls) explains a modest part of the variance of taste for inequality, about 5.4 percent in the best of the equations. Second, there is clearly an increase in explanatory power between 2000 and 2008, between a twofold and threefold increase in explanatory power which is visible for both income and social status. This would suggest that Egyptians became much more sensitive to income and social class when they express their views about inequality, which is a finding consistent with previous findings on the dual mode distribution of satisfaction and with the changes in inequality aversion across income

Table 3.9 Taste for Inequality Regressions (OLS)

	(1)	(2)		(3)	(4)
Variables	2000	2008	Variables	2000	2008
Income scale 2[a]	0.0504	−0.0517	working class[c]	0.0679	−0.0650
	(0.137)	(0.129)		(0.132)	(0.156)
Income scale 3[a]	0.00750	0.0577	lower-middle class[c]	0.0436	0.255*
	(0.133)	(0.138)		(0.114)	(0.135)
Income scale 4[a]	−0.0105	0.519**	upper-middle class[c]	0.241*	0.577***
	(0.138)	(0.214)		(0.141)	(0.198)
Income scale 5[a]	0.127	1.107**	upper class[c]	0.916**	1.828***
	(0.176)	(0.470)		(0.414)	(0.560)
Savings last 12 months	0.230*	0.724***	Savings last 12 months	0.152	0.575**
	(0.124)	(0.221)		(0.121)	(0.233)
Sex	0.0744	−0.00132	Sex	0.0126	0.00991
	(0.0919)	(0.134)		(0.0897)	(0.133)
Age	−0.00909	0.0385*	Age	0.00558	0.0404*
	(0.0176)	(0.0227)		(0.0168)	(0.0226)
Age squared	0.000207	−0.000357	Age squared	1.41e-05	−0.000378
	(0.000190)	(0.000240)		(0.000183)	(0.000239)
Married	0.221**	0.0887	Married	0.130	0.0736
	(0.104)	(0.134)		(0.102)	(0.134)
No. of children	−0.0560**	−0.0629*	No. of children	−0.0406	−0.0638*
	(0.0263)	(0.0331)		(0.0263)	(0.0331)
Secondary education[d]	0.00295	0.447***	Secondary education	−0.0202	0.395***
	(0.0999)	(0.120)		(0.0993)	(0.121)
Tertiary education[d]	0.116	0.480***	Tertiary education	0.0602	0.379**
	(0.123)	(0.171)		(0.121)	(0.173)
Full-time employment	−0.0245	0.200	Full-time employment	−0.0562	0.242*
	(0.0998)	(0.138)		(0.0973)	(0.138)
Town size < = 50,000	−0.0273	0.0369	Town size < = 50,000	−0.0543	0.0474
	(0.160)	(0.103)		(0.152)	(0.102)
Alexandria[b]	0.243	1.224***	Alexandria[b]	0.255	1.303***
	(0.183)	(0.243)		(0.177)	(0.243)
Lower Egypt[b]	−0.0707	0.827***	Lower Egypt[b]	−0.0999	0.879***
	(0.207)	(0.165)		(0.196)	(0.164)
Upper Egypt[b]	−0.119	0.170	Upper Egypt[b]	−0.0805	0.225
	(0.193)	(0.170)		(0.183)	(0.169)
Others[b]	0.507**	1.176***	Others[b]	0.531**	1.216***
	(0.214)	(0.307)		(0.207)	(0.307)
Constant	8.150***	4.997***	Constant	7.949***	4.794***
	(0.387)	(0.542)		(0.370)	(0.543)
Observations	2,667	3,007	Observations	2,883	3,009
R-squared	0.019	0.051	R-squared	0.020	0.054

Source: WVS 2000 and 2008.

Note: Standard errors in parentheses. OLS = ordinary least squares. WVS = World Values Survey.

*** p<0.01, ** p<0.05, * p<0.1.

a. Base category: Income scale 1.

b. Base category: Cairo.

c. Base category: Lower class.

d. Base category: Primary education.

classes. Third, social class is more important than income class when it comes to judging inequality. In 2000, the two upper-social class variables are significant while none of the income class variables are significant. In 2008, the three upper classes for social class are significant while for income is only the two upper classes, and coefficients and significance are higher for the social class variables as compared to the income variables. Views on inequality seem to be more strongly rooted in social classes than in income classes.

The recent household performance (savings) is also important in explaining the taste for inequality and the importance of this variable increases between 2000 and 2008 for both the income and the social class equations. The size of the town does not seem to make a difference but the regional location becomes very important in 2008. People living in Alexandria and Lower Egypt seem to have developed a greater taste for inequality as compared to people living in Cairo. Again, this could be interpreted as people gaining more awareness of the differences between welfare across regions as seen before between income classes. It is also interesting to note that the number of children increases inequality aversion while people with higher education are less inequality averse, both factors being more important in 2008 than in 2000.

Overall, the findings outlined on welfare and the perceptions of welfare converge in telling a consistent story. Between 2000 and 2008, Egyptians have experienced a radical change in perceptions about welfare and inequality with differences across income classes, social classes, and regions increasing in importance. In other words, the revolution in perceptions was already occurring throughout the decade that preceded the 2011 revolution and an attentive look into these data might have provided a different picture from the one portrayed by GDP growth alone.

Coming back to our central question on the perception of inequality, it is also instructive to put Egypt in comparative perspective with other countries. Figure 3.16 compares the average change in appreciation of inequality across the sample of countries that were surveyed by the WVSs in both the fourth and fifth rounds (around 2000 and around 2008). The WVSs today cover more than ninety countries but for this specific comparison we wanted to use countries that were surveyed during the same period of time and with the same questions covered by the Egyptian surveys so that these countries would be subject to the same global changes. This reduced the sample to the 19 countries depicted in figure 3.16.

It is immediately evident that the countries where the reduction in the appreciation for inequality has been the greatest are all Middle East and North Africa countries including Morocco, the Islamic Republic of Iran, and Egypt with Jordan also in the negative block. In the group of countries that show a reduction in the appreciation for inequality we also find Moldova, China, Vietnam, and Peru. If we were to interpret these results in terms of GDP growth, we would not find any relation between the appreciation of inequality and growth. All emerging economies shown in the figure have gone through a period of sustained growth between 2000 and 2008, and we find countries with exceptional growth that are situated on both sides of the figure. For example, China and Vietnam show very significant drops in the appreciation of inequality while India and Turkey show

Figure 3.16 Average Change in the Taste for Inequality, 2000–08

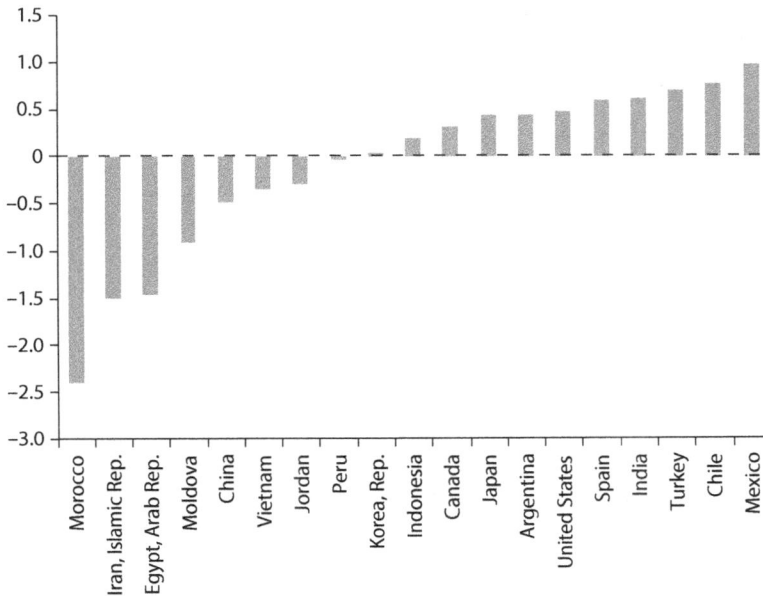

Source: WVSs 2000, 2008.
Note: WVS = World Values Surveys.

large increases despite the fact that all these countries experienced exceptional growth during the period. It would be hard to explain such changes in attitudes toward inequality in terms of growth alone as suggested by some of the theoretical literature reviewed.

By contrast, it is evident that the countries in the positive block are all democracies with no exceptions while the countries in the negative block are all political systems that can be described to different degrees as nondemocratic with the sole exceptions of Moldova and Peru. While all emerging economies depicted in figure 3.16 have experienced sustained growth during the decade considered, the emerging economies that are not full democracies show a drop in the appreciation of inequality. As the countries selected were not handpicked but simply those for which data were available during the period, it would be difficult to reduce such finding to simple randomness or self-selection. There seems to be a relation between political institutions and the appreciation of inequality during periods of growth.

If we look at other key variables for a society such as freedom and control and trust in other people (figure 3.17) we see that the countries where the taste for inequality has decreased are also countries that have not done very well in terms of these other variables. For example, while Turkey and South Africa tend to be on the positive scale on all indicators with a greatest appreciation for inequality followed by greater life satisfaction, freedom and control, and trust, Morocco and Egypt tend to be on the negative side of the scales or mildly positive. This relation between the taste for inequality, freedom, and trust is not univocal but could

Figure 3.17 Average Changes in Key Perceptions Variables, 2000–08

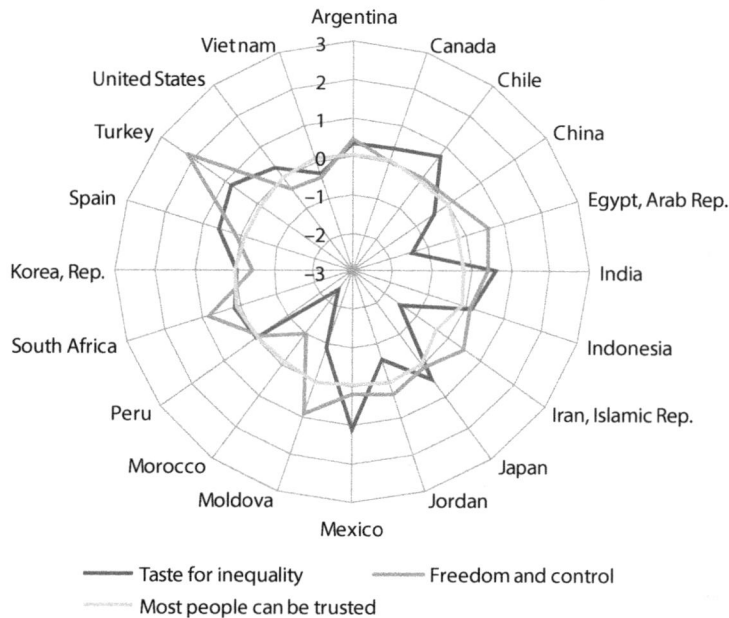

——— Taste for inequality   ——— Freedom and control
·········· Most people can be trusted

Source: WVSs 2000, 2008.

suggest that people value more inequality if in the presence of increased freedom, trust, and democratic institutions.

As we learned from the brief review on the empirical literature that looked at the relation between inequality and perceptions of inequality many factors seem to drive perceptions on inequality which may be unrelated or weakly related to inequality itself. One of these factors is political orientations. For example, Alesina et al. (2004) found that North Americans have typically a higher taste for inequality than Europeans but also found that the taste for inequality is very much associated with political orientation anywhere with left-wing voters having a lower appreciation of inequality than right-wing voters. Religion is a second factor that is very important in explaining perceptions on a wide range of factors and, especially in countries where religion plays an important role in every aspect of life, this factor could also affect perceptions of inequality. Both Islam and Christianity, the two dominant religions in Egypt, profess equality and the care of the poor and destitutes as fundamental values. The WVSs provide a number of variables that measure political and religious views, and we used these variables as regressors in a taste for inequality equation. The results are shown in table 3.10.

People with greater interest in politics seem to have a greater appreciation of inequality and this was true in 2000 as in 2008. By contrast, people who think that is very good or fairly good to have a strong political leader have a lower appreciation of inequality than people with opposite views. In 2000, people who thought was important to have a good democratic political system did not have strong preferences for inequality, but this variable becomes significant in 2008

Table 3.10 Politics and Religion

Variables	(1) 2000	(2) 2008
Very or somewhat interested in politics	0.253***	0.267**
	(0.0800)	(0.110)
Very good or fairly good to have a strong leader	−0.384***	−0.945***
	(0.147)	(0.140)
Very good to have a democratic political system	0.0761	0.220*
	(0.0805)	(0.124)
Attend religious premises at least once a week	0.0408	−0.360***
	(0.0761)	(0.132)
Religious institutions give answers to people's spiritual needs	0.497***	−0.0653
	(0.148)	(0.110)
Christian	0.0553	−0.117
	(0.165)	(0.208)
Controls	Yes	yes
Constant	7.518***	5.208***
	(0.385)	(0.574)
Observations	2,882	2,941
R-squared	0.027	0.062

Source: WVS 2000, 2008.
Note: Standard errors in parentheses. Controls: Sex, age, marital status, number of children, education, full-time employment, city size, and region.
*** $p<0.01$, ** $p<0.05$, * $p<0.1$.

and with a positive sign suggesting that views on higher inequality are associated with views about good democratic systems. For all these political variables the degree of significance increases across the two years considered.

In terms of religion, those who actually practice religion by attending religious premises at least once a week did not have any particular preference for inequality in 2000 but developed a lower taste for inequality between 2000 and 2008 as compared to those who do not practice religion regularly. Trust in religious institutions as providers of spiritual guidance was a factor that in 2000 was associated with greater appreciation of inequality, but this variable is no longer significant in 2008. When we looked at the four questions of the WVSs related to trust in the religious institutions in providing answers to various needs (moral, spiritual, family, and social needs), we found a very sharp fall in trust for all the four needs between 2000 and 2008. Apparently, Egyptians became much more disillusioned with the capacity of the religious institutions to provide support to people and this is not related to people's practice of religion as the number of goers between the two years has slightly increased. Therefore, practicing religion leads to more inequality aversion but this is unrelated to perception on the role of religious institutions in society. Interestingly, there is no difference between Christians and Muslims in the average appreciation of inequality.

There are other views of people that may help understanding how inequality is perceived. Sentiments on freedom for example that have been voiced during the 2011 revolution in Egypt may be expected to be related to the judgment on inequality but also feelings of trust, attitudes toward work, and opinions about gender roles are other aspects recurrently mentioned in the specific literature that could help to better interpret views on inequality. Results of the taste of inequality regressions with these variables are shown in table 3.11.

As it is well known in happiness research, the variable freedom and control is the best explanatory factor of life satisfaction worldwide. This variable captures feelings of freedom of choice combined with feelings of being in control of one's own life.[8] In our equation, this variable is not significant for 2000 but becomes very significant in 2008 with people feeling greater freedom and control having a better appreciation of higher inequality with both the significance level and the coefficient being very high. Trust is also a nonsignificant variable in 2000 but becomes very significant in 2008 with a negative sign suggesting that people who have great trust in others became more inequality averse during the period 2000–08. During this period, the share of people who declared to trust most people declined by half which means that those who became less trusty over the period are also those who had a greater appreciation of inequality in 2000.

People who think that work is very important and that is never justifiable cheating on taxes are clearly pro-inequality with these variables being positive and significant in both years considered. This could be interpreted as honest and hardworking people expecting to be rewarded for such efforts with higher incomes leading to higher inequality. The period 2000–08 has also sharpened these feelings. Gender views are also clearly related to views on inequality. Those

Table 3.11 Freedom, Trust, Cheating, Work, and Gender Role

Variables	2000	2008
Feel free and in control	−0.0980	0.760***
	(0.0753)	(0.101)
Most people can be trusted	0.0395	−0.709***
	(0.0782)	(0.128)
Never justifiable to cheat on taxes	0.404***	0.517***
	(0.0943)	(0.117)
Work is very important	0.321***	0.251**
	(0.0915)	(0.117)
University is more important for a boy than for a girl	−0.281***	−0.206*
	(0.107)	(0.114)
Controls	yes	yes
Constant	7.721***	4.345***
	(0.370)	(0.546)
Observations	2,985	3,010
R-squared	0.030	0.079

Source: WVS 2000 and 2008.
Note: Standard errors in parentheses. Controls: Sex, age, marital status, number of children, education, full-time employment, city size, and region.
*** $p<0.01$, ** $p<0.05$, * $p<0.1$.

who have strong feelings about university education being more important for boys rather than girls are also those more inequality averse as we find a negative and significant sign in both years. This is perhaps a view that signals conservative and religious views about gender roles but that is also clearly associated with inequality aversion.[9]

Summary and Conclusions

The paper has researched one of the puzzling aspects of contemporary Egypt, namely the apparent mismatch between income inequality measured by household surveys (HIECS surveys 2000, 2005, 2009) and the perception of income inequality measured by values surveys (WVSs 2000, 2008).

The analysis started by reviewing and validating the facts about the measurement of income inequality with the HIECS data. Following a discussion on data quality, we reconstructed comparable welfare aggregates over the years and found the HIECS to be a good and consistent household survey. The main problem for the measurement of inequality is not the quality of the data *per se* but the fact that CAPMAS typically provides to researchers only 25 percent of the full sample, and this can result in variations in the measurement of inequality of two–three percentage points. Despite this shortcoming, the paper was able to establish with a good degree of statistical accuracy a number of facts on welfare and inequality:

- Household welfare in real terms has not improved overall between 2000 and 2009 and has declined for most households.
- Poorer households have performed relatively better than richer households between 2000 and 2009. However, almost 50 percent of households have experienced at least one poverty spell between 2005 and 2009.
- The gap between GDP per capita and household consumption has increased during the last decade. While GDP per capita has grown steadily, household consumption has not increased.
- Inequality has not increased between 2000 and 2009. The estimated statistics show a decline in the Gini coefficient, which is consistent for income and expenditure and also consistent with previous studies. Statistical considerations indicate that these declines are not robust but it is possible to conclude with a good degree of statistical accuracy that inequality has not increased. A recent paper by Hlasny and Verme (2013) has reinforced these results.
- In 2009, the level of expenditure inequality estimated at around 33 percent was low by international and regional standards.
- A missing values analysis shows no evidence of richer households self-selecting themselves out of the sample.
- Income inequality is mostly driven by wages and interhouseholds transfers. Expenditure inequality is mostly driven by expenditure on services.

In the light of these facts about welfare and income inequality how have people's perceptions changed in relation to welfare and income inequality? The paper was able to determine a number of insights about people's perceptions:

- The 2000–08 period saw a remarkable change in people's perceptions on a vast range of issues. A possible explanation seems to be an increased awareness of the population about economic and social issues and a better sense on the part of households of their own relative position in society.
- People's priorities changed from general views about freedom and the environment to very concrete aspirations about GDP growth and stable food prices.
- There is a clear decline in self-reported incomes and social status. In 2008, households felt poorer than in 2000 and they felt that they belonged to a lower social stratum.
- Between 2000 and 2008, the mismatch between actual welfare and welfare expectations increased.
- There is an evident sharp rise in inequality aversion for almost all income groups and all social groups.
- Poorer people have grown more inequality averse than richer people despite a relatively better performance over the period.
- Social class is more important than incomes in explaining aversion to income inequality.
- Internationally, there seems to be a negative correlation between the degree of democratization and the growth of inequality aversion during periods of GDP growth while there is no direct association between GDP growth and inequality aversion.
- Inequality aversion is also positively associated with freedom and interest in politics and negatively associated with trust and religious practice.

The analysis of facts and perceptions of inequality has largely confirmed the initial puzzle. Income inequality measured with HIECS surveys is effectively low and not a statistical artifact while people have grown more inequality averse as suggested by media reports. Therefore, the paradox of the mismatch between facts and perceptions of inequality fully stands after our investigation. The question now is how to explain the paradox. The paper has provided a number of important leads that can help to answer this question which can be summarized as follows:

1. *Growth and volatility have changed people's expectations.* Between 2000 and 2009 Egypt has experienced a period of sustained GDP growth and also increased volatility, especially in food and commodity prices. Theory suggests that during such periods people change expectations and this is what we found with the World Values Surveys (WVSs). Egyptians became more worried about issues such as GDP growth and food prices.
2. *People became more socially and economically aware.* We found very significant changes in the distributions of a number of key variables such as life

satisfaction, trust, freedom, people's priorities, and also inequality aversion. It is as if people became more aware of their relative conditions and expressed this new awareness through changes in views on a broad range of topics.

3. *Absolute household welfare has declined for most households.* Even when inequality increases, households may still show greater levels of satisfaction if, overall, their own situation improves. But this was not the case in Egypt and people can hardly appreciate inequality if their own status and the status of their peers do not improve.

4. *GDP has not trickled down to households.* While GDP growth may have filled the pages of newspapers, back home household welfare was not improving as documented by the HIECS. Instead, most of the GDP growth accrued to private enterprises and mostly retained or exported. This lack of direct gains from growth must have frustrated households and contributed to shape household opinions on income inequality.

5. *The perceived decline in welfare was greater than the actual decline in welfare.* This was documented with the WVS for both incomes and social class and complies with the fact that people became more socially and economically aware.

6. *The mismatch between actual welfare and expected welfare has increased.* This is a natural consequence of the two points above. Egyptians were poorer at the end of the decade as compared to the beginning of the decade but felt even poorer as compared to the actual situation. As suggested by theory, this mismatch is a very strong driver of perceptions about welfare.

7. *Lack of democratic institutions may sharpen adversity to inequality.* We saw that among growing economies less democratic states experienced a sharper growth in inequality aversion. This is not conclusive evidence but an interesting lead for future research.

8. *Change in the reference group.* As discussed in the brief theoretical review, social sciences have long ago established the importance of the reference group in determining self-assessed well-being. The reference group is generally defined as the group of people perceived as peers and that individuals use to compare themselves with to self-assess status in society. The expansion of Internet-based social networks has clearly changed the reference group in two directions. It has expanded the reference group to encompass a much larger number of people and has broken the national boundaries of the reference group. Through social networks, people gained more peers and peers abroad, across the Middle East and North Africa region and outside the Middle East and North Africa region. By changing the reference group, self-assessed status in society changes and so do expectations and aspirations, which is what we observed in the WVSs. This growth in aspirations and expectations generated by cross-country comparisons in the face of no growth in income or opportunities at home may well explain in part the mismatch between observed inequality and perceived inequality.

While the culprits of our initial puzzle may not have been found, the paper has provided a number of strong leads to explain the mismatch between facts and perceptions of income inequality. Neither the data nor the people have been found to be wrong. On the contrary, in the light of the evidence provided in this paper, we could argue that there is no puzzle and that people's perceptions are consistent with the facts if we are willing to broaden the factual analysis beyond the statistical measurement of income inequality.

References

Alesina, A., R. Di Tella, and R. MacCulloch. 2004. "Inequality and Happiness: Are Europeans and Americans Different?" *Journal of Public Economics* 88: 2009–42.

Clark, A. E. 2003. "Inequality Aversion and Income Mobility: A Direct Test." Delta Working Papers, 11, Paris, France.

Davies, J. C. 1962. "Toward a Theory of Revolution." *American Sociological Review* 27 (1): 5–19.

Davis, J. A. 1959. "A Formal Interpretation of the Theory of Relative Deprivation." *Sociometry* 22 (4): 280–96.

Graham, C., and A. Felton. 2006. "Inequality and Happiness: Insights from Latin America." *Journal of Economic Inequality* 4 (1): 107–22.

Gurr, T. 1968. "A Causal Model of Civil Strife: A Comparative Analysis Using New Indices." *The American Political Science Review* 62 (4): 1104–24.

Hirschman, A. O., and M. Rothschild. 1973. "The Changing Tolerance for Income Inequality in the Course of Economic Development." *The Quarterly Journal of Economics* 87 (4): 544–66.

Hlasny, V., and P. Verme. 2013. "Top Incomes and the Measurement of Inequality in Egypt" Policy Research Working Paper No. 6557, World Bank, Washington, DC.

Karapetoff, W.(1903. "On Life Satisfaction." *The American Journal of Sociology* 8 (5): 681–86.

Marotta, D., R. Yemtsov, H. El-Laithy, H. Abou-Ali, and S. Al-Shawarby. 2011. "Was Growth in Egypt Between 2005 and 2008 Pro-Poor From Static to Dynamic Poverty Profile." Policy Research Working Paper 3068, World Bank, Washington, DC.

Morawetz, D., E. Atia, G. Bin-Nun, L. Felous, Y. Gariplerden, E. Harris, S. Soustiel, G. Tombros, and Y. Zarfaty. 1977. "Income Distribution and Self-Rated Happiness: Some Empirical Evidence." *Economic Journal* 87: 511–22.

Runciman, W. G. 1966. "Relative Deprivation and Social Justice." Reports of the Institute of Community Studies. Routledge and Kegan Paul, London, Boston and Henley.

Senik, C. 2004. "When Information Dominates Comparison. Learning from Russian Subjective Panel Data." *Journal of Public Economics* 88: 2099–133.

Veenhoven, R. 1996. "Happy Life Expectancy. A Comprehensive Measure of Quality-of-Life in Nations." *Social Indicators Research* 39: 1–58.

Verme, P. 2009. "Happiness, Freedom and Control." *Journal of Economic Behavior & Organization* 71: 146–61.

———. 2011. "Life Satisfaction and Income Inequality." *Review of Income and Wealth* 57 (1): 111–37.

Yitzhaki, S. 1979. "Relative Deprivation and the Gini Coefficient." *Quarterly Journal of Economics* 93: 321–24.

World Bank. 2007. "Arab Republic of Egypt, Poverty Assessment Update." Report No. 39885 – EG, Vols 1 and 2, Washington, DC.

———. 2011. "Arab Republic of Egypt. Poverty in Egypt 2008–09." Report No. 60249-EG, Washington, DC.

Notes

1. Note that we refer to *changes* in the capacity to capture the two tails of the distribution rather than the capacity itself which is not discussed here.

2. It should be noted that inequality decompositions can be conducted only with non-empty observations. Therefore, missing observations are replaced with zeroes on the assumption that households who did not answer questions on certain components of income or expenditure do not have these components. For example, agricultural income that pertains mainly to rural households will carry a value of zero for all empty observations.

3. It should be noted that the WVSs are implemented over short periods of time, typically during a few weeks. Given that these surveys capture opinions, these opinions can be influenced by the particular situation of the moment and what ranks high in the press and public debates, for example.

4. Explanations on these surveys with details on samples, methodology, and questionnaires can be found online at http://www.worldvaluessurvey.org/.

5. This may seem in contrast to the main demands heard during the occupation of Tahir square, but we should not neglect that the information used in this paper comes from a representative sample of the population while it is largely unknown whether the population in Tahir square was effectively a representative sample of the whole population or a bias sample of selected groups.

6. Note that for this exercise the 1 to 10 income scale was reduced to 5 steps for comparing the answers with the social class question.

7. With a categorical ordered dependent variable as the one we use, a multinomial logit model would have been more appropriate. However, given the small size of the sample and the ten categories used for the dependent variable, it becomes very difficult to detect significance. By using an OLS model we are assuming that the variable taste for inequality is linear in the ten steps considered and that the ten steps are equidistant. This is not an unreasonable assumption, given the formulation of the question.

8. Verme (2009) shows how this variable is the most powerful predictor of life satisfaction worldwide and also shows how the two aspects of freedom and control boost each other in explaining life satisfaction.

9. Note that all respondents, males and females, replied to the question and that among the controls (not reported in the table) we also have a dummy for gender.

CHAPTER 4

Poverty and Inequality in the Arab Republic of Egypt's Poorest Villages

Sahar El Tawila, May Gadallah, and Enas Ali A.El-Majeed

Introduction

Identifying the determinants of inequality has recently been considered an imperative first step to formulate effective policies aiming at poverty reduction (Wan 2002; Wan 2004; Wan and Zhou 2004, 2005; Kimhi 2007; Naschold 2010). Poverty and inequality are two related concepts, but they are not synonymous. Poverty refers to: "Those who live below a reasonable minimum standard of living," which can be measured in monetary or nonmonetary[1] terms. Monetary poverty lines entail insufficiency of income, expenditure, or consumption to cover basic food and nonfood needs. For international comparisons the US$1.25 and US$2.50 per person per day standards are helpful, while for targeting the poor a country-specific poverty line is required. This is typically the "National Lower Poverty Line," in short "the poverty line," which represents the cost of the minimum subsistence basket comprising food along with nonfood goods and services.[2]

While poverty is concerned only by the population below a certain threshold, inequality is defined over the entire population, and addresses the differences in the income/expenditure/or consumption distribution. Inequality looks at variations in the standards of living across a whole population and implicitly points to deprivation in terms of income, assets, health and nutrition, education, social inclusion, power, and security. Inequality usually relates to population profiles characterized by a majority of poor and a small middle class, or when the society has a considerably larger middle class that has distanced itself from the poor (Coudouel et al. 2002). Three main measures of inequality are usually used; the Gini coefficient,[3] the ratio of actual consumption of the 80th percentile to the actual consumption of the 20th percentile,[4] and the percent share of actual consumption of the first quintile in total actual consumption. The latter is the third indicator of the first goal among the Millennium Development Goals (MDGs).

Poverty analysis in Egypt is conventionally based on household actual consumption rather than income. National statistics based upon the results of the 2008/09 and 2010/11 rounds of the Egypt's Households Income, Expenditure and Consumption Surveys (HIECS) showed that 22 percent and 25 percent of all Egyptians in 2008/09 and in 2010/11 respectively were below the poverty line. Slightly less than 7 percent and 5 percent in the two rounds, respectively, were considered ultra poor; that is, below the food poverty line. Poverty in Egypt is mainly a rural phenomenon, particularly in Upper Egypt. In 2008/09, the incidence of poverty in rural areas was 2.4 times that in urban regions; 28 percent of residents in rural areas were below the poverty line; 17 percent in rural Lower Egypt and 44 percent in rural Upper Egypt. Comparable statistics from the 2010/11 round of the HIECS were: 2.1 times, 32.3 percent, 16.8 percent and 50.7 percent.

Despite the prevalence of higher poverty rates in rural areas, inequality in rural Egypt is lower than the overall average in the country. Using the distribution of actual consumption in 2008/09, the 80/20 ratio was equal to 4.5 for total Egypt; hence, the average person of the richest 20 percent of the population consumed 4.5 times as much as the average person of the poorest 20 percent. The comparable ratio in total rural Egypt was 3.1 only. In 2008/09, the National Gini coefficient was 31.5, compared to 22.4 in rural Egypt. In 2010/11, the National Gini coefficient was 31.6, compared to 23.9 in rural Egypt.

Within the context of the Government of Egypt initiative to develop the poorest 1,000 villages, a household-based survey was conducted around the same time as the HIECS round of 2008/09 and availed a unique data set representative of the poorest 20 percent of villages in Egypt; that is, the very left tail of the household income/consumption distribution in all villages in rural Egypt. The data collected were representative at the community/village level and also at the level of the households in these communities.

This study has two main objectives: (i) To assess the level of poverty and inequality in the poorest villages in Egypt and, to examine how these compare to the level of poverty and inequality in total Egypt and in total rural Egypt; (ii) To investigate the relationship between poverty and inequality as well as the determinants of both poverty and inequality in the poorest villages in Egypt.

The importance of the study is not only due to the use of data pertaining to some of the most impoverished local communities in Egypt and to the use of household level data in addition to aggregate community/village data in analyzing inequality but also in attempting to quantify the contribution of each of these determinants to the inequality in poor rural Egypt.

The Government of Egypt Initiative to Develop the Poorest 1,000 Villages and Related M&E System

In 2007, the Government of Egypt (GoE) declared its intention to target the poorest 1,000 villages[5] with a significant level of investment in an integrated package of basic services. The initiative aimed to create a sustained improved livelihood for the residents of these 1,000 villages, reducing poverty and vulnerability of the most unprivileged groups in these villages. According to the poverty map (2007), almost one-half of the population of these poorest 1,000 villages were classified as poor (figure 4.1).

Figure 4.1 Egypt Villages Distribution by Poverty Rate

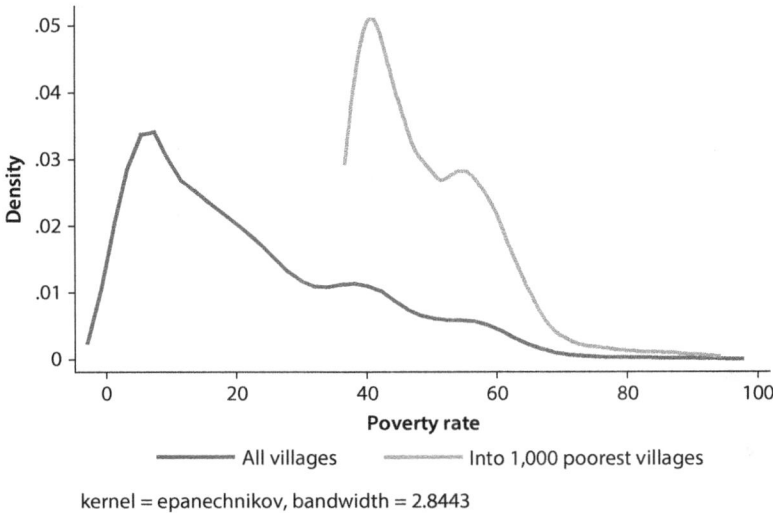

kernel = epanechnikov, bandwidth = 2.8443

Source: World Bank data using The Egyptian poverty map 2007 (based on HIECS 2004/05, and Census 2006).

The Egyptian government embarked on implementation of Phase I of the initiative in 151 villages. These villages are administratively located in 24 local units in the six governorates of Sharqia and, Behera (both in Lower Upper), and Menia, Assiut, Sohag, and Qena (in Upper Egypt). Of the 151 villages only 108 villages belong to the poorest 1,000 villages. In the meantime, the Social Contract Center of Egypt developed a Monitoring and Evaluation (M&E) System to provide evidence-based programmatic and policy advice with regard to the effectiveness, efficiency, equity, and sustainability of the government initiative. The proposed research design for the evaluation of the impact of the government initiative was both a "before and after" and a "with and without intervention" design. The intervention group comprised all 151 villages included in Phase I of the government initiative. The control group comprised 35 villages in the six governorates where the government initiative was implemented. Unlike the intervention villages, all control villages except two belong to the list of the 1,000 poorest villages. In each of the six governorates, the overall community and population characteristics in the control villages matched the overall community and population characteristics in the intervention villages in that particular governorate.

The Baseline Study of the M&E System

Among the proposed components of the M&E system was a quantitative baseline survey implemented in December 2009/January 2010 in all 151 intervention villages as well as in the 35 control villages. The proposed sampling design was a simple stratified probability sampling design aimed to minimize the standard errors of all estimates obtained from the sample. Two levels of stratification were relevant in this context: the governorate level (six strata corresponding to the six governorates), and within governorates, the communities/villages were divided into two main strata, namely mother villages and other (not a mother village).[6] Mother villages typically have a larger population size and relatively easier access to public services compared to other villages.

A community questionnaire was filled out for each village. The subsections of the questionnaire primarily measured the population size, agricultural land, and environment-related indicators, in addition to the availability of public services in the village and the level of utilization of available services.

The household survey questionnaire collected information on:

1. Characteristics of all household members: age, sex, education and work status, disability, and chronic health conditions
2. Detailed information on household income from different sources
3. Household access to infrastructure, housing conditions, possession of durable goods, and economic assets
4. Aggregate information on household expenditures on food and nonfood items during the relevant recall periods
5. Access to and perception of the quality of public services: water, sanitation, education, literacy classes, health, roads, social assistance, micro credit, and others.

Data on both the intervention and control villages that were not among the poorest 1,000 villages (43 intervention villages and two control villages) were excluded from this analysis. Data utilized in this analysis comprise the remaining 141 villages (108 intervention villages and 33 control villages) combined together. The decision to combine the data of all 141 villages was based on the clear evidence provided by both figure 4.2 and figure 4.3 indicating that both

Figure 4.2 Natural Logarithm (Ln) Consumption/Capita for Intervention and Control Villages

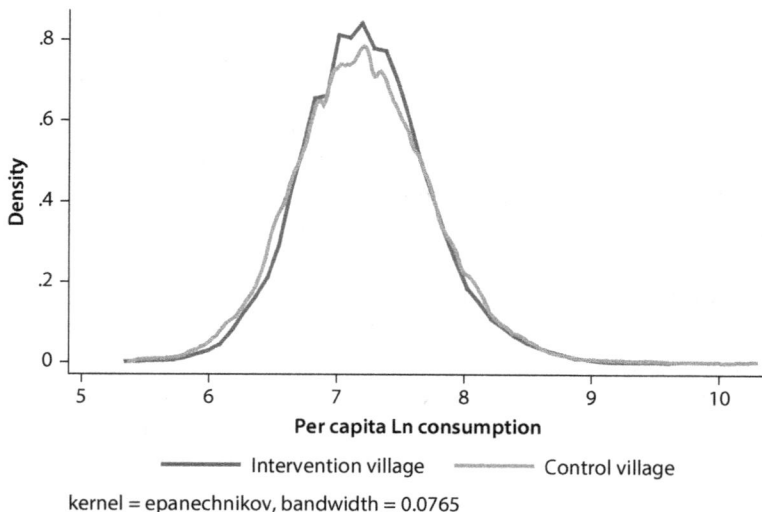

kernel = epanechnikov, bandwidth = 0.0765

Source: Calculated by the authors, out of the baseline survey of the 1,000 Poorest Villages Intervention.

Figure 4.3 Natural Logarithm (Ln) Consumption/Capita for Mother and Nonmother Villages

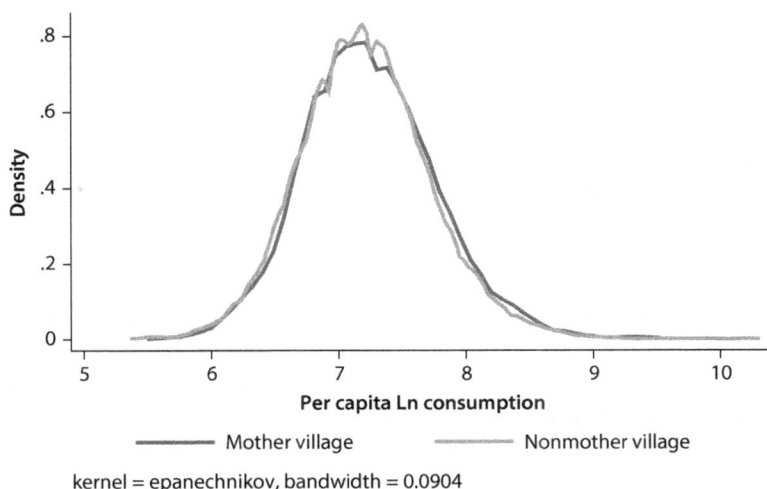

kernel = epanechnikov, bandwidth = 0.0904

Source: Calculated by the authors, out of the baseline survey of the 1,000 Poorest Villages Intervention.

intervention and control villages—as well as mother and nonmother villages—have income and consumption distributions that are identical.

Poverty rankings of the 141 villages are almost uniformly distributed among the poorest 1,000 villages in Egypt starting with the village with the 47th rank and ending with the village with the 998th rank. The total number of sampled households from these 141 villages amounts to 10,568 households.

Poverty in the Poorest Villages of Egypt

Actual per capita household consumption[7] was used to estimate poverty measures in the 141 poorest villages.[8] Results of the baseline household survey in the 141 villages revealed that around 81.7 percent of residents in these villages were poor; that is, they could not satisfy all their food and nonfood basic needs. Moreover, 64.9 percent of residents in these villages were ultra poor and could not satisfy even their basic food needs only.

Toward the end of 2009, a person in Egypt was considered poor if she/he spent on average less than LE 197 per month (LE 2,364 per year) and those who spent less than LE 148 per month (LE 1,776 per year) were considered ultra poor. Findings from the data indicate that the average monthly per capita consumption in the 141 villages was only LE 131 (LE 1,572 per year), less than the threshold to escape extreme poverty (LE 148 per month/LE 1,776 per year). Furthermore, unlike the overall shallow nature of poverty in Egypt (where most of the poor cluster around the poverty line), poverty in these particular villages is deep. The poverty gap index[9] was 35.3 percent compared to 5.9 percent at the level of total rural Egypt (see table 4.1).

It is worthwhile to mention in this regard that the large discrepancy in the level of poverty between total rural Egypt and the study villages should

Table 4.1 Poverty Measures from Egypt Households Income, Expenditure and Consumption Survey (HIECS) in 2008/09 and in the 141 Study Villages

	HIECS data 2008/09*		
Poverty measure	Egypt	Rural Egypt	141 study villages**
Total poor (%)	22	28	81.7
Total ultra poor (%)	7	-	64.9
Poverty gap index	4.2	5.9	35.3

Source: (*) HIECS 2008/09 Report, by Central Agency for Public Mobilization and Statistics (CAPMAS); (**) Calculated by the authors.

be assessed in the light of two facts. First, the 141 villages selectively belong to the poorest 20 percent of all villages in the country, and second, the methodology used for collecting the consumption data is different between the HIECS and the baseline survey in the poorest villages. In the HIECS, household consumption data were collected in great detail over the course of one month and per item consumed on a daily basis, using a diary system. In the baseline survey, the household consumption per month was collected just once using one question per category for each of the main categories of consumption. We believe that while the difference in the methodologies used for collecting consumption data—and for imputations of the housing expenses/rent—may indeed have contributed to widening the gap between the poverty estimates from the two surveys, the fact that the majority of households in the poorest villages initially had very low levels of income combined with the very limited consumption options available in these villages and the low levels of housing rents would not allow for either significant imputation errors or recall errors concerning their consumption. Of course that would not have been the case had the focus been on households with higher levels of income and consumption, residing in communities having a wider access to more variable options for consumption and higher levels of housing rents.

Table 4.2 displays the mean annual per capita consumption (and related 95 percent confidence interval) within quintiles of the consumption distribution and by poverty status in the study villages compared to total Egypt and total rural Egypt.

The mean per capita consumption per year in the study villages is systematically 50 percent less than the corresponding mean per capita for total Egypt in all quintiles. The mean per capita consumption per year in the third quintile in the study villages barely matches (indeed remain less than) the mean per capita consumption per year in the first quintile in total rural Egypt. And while the mean annual per capita consumption by poverty status is identical in total rural Egypt and in total Egypt, the corresponding figures in the study villages are 30 percent less than both in each category. These results are quite indicative of a profile in the poorest villages characterized by

Table 4.2 Mean Per Capita Consumption/Year within Quintiles and by Poverty Status in Study Villages, in Total Egypt, and in Total Rural Egypt

	Mean per capita consumption/year 95% confidence interval		
	HIECS data 2008/09*		
	Egypt	Rural Egypt	141 study villages**
Quintiles			
Q1	1714	1593.8	716.8
	1711.1 1716.9	1590.5 1597.2	713.8 719.8
Q2	2423.5	2207.3	1083.6
	2422.1 2425.2	2205.6 2208.9	1081.6 1085.5
Q3	3032.6	2681.8	1379
	3030.8 3034.4	2680.0 2683.5	1376.8 1381.1
Q4	3887	3257.1	1761.2
	3883.9 3890.1	3254.7 3259.6	1757.8 1764.5
Q5	7503.6	4883.4	3034.6
	7456.3 7551.0	4857.4 4909.5	3004.0 3065.3
Poverty Status			
Nonpoor	4246	3396.1	2955.4
	4230.6 4261.4	3386.2 3406.1	2920.3 2990.6
Poor			
Inclusive of ultra poor	1821.4	1823.6	1266
	1817.8 1824.9	1819.5 1827.6	1260.9 1271.2
Ultra poor only	1416.1	1427.1	1105.7
	1411.7 1420.5	1422.3 1432.0	1101.4 1110.1

Source: (*) HIECS 2008/09 Report, by Central Agency for Public Mobilization and Statistics (CAPMAS); (**) Calculated by the authors.

a very large majority of poor households and a small middle class: a situation usually conducive to higher levels of inequality.

Inequality in the Poorest Villages in Egypt

Figure 4.4 displays the two distributions of the natural logarithm (Ln) of both household per capita income and household per capita actual consumption of all 10,568 households in the study villages. It shows that the distribution of the natural logarithm of household per capita consumption is less variable and more clustered around the mean, compared to the distribution of the natural logarithm of household per capita income that is less clustered around the mean and more spread toward the two tails.

Using the distribution of actual consumption in the study villages, the 80/20 ratio is equal to 3.9; hence the average person of the richest 20 percent of the population in these villages consumes 3.9 times as much as the average person of the poorest 20 percent compared to 4.5 times in total Egypt and 3.1 in total

Figure 4.4 Natural Logarithm Distributions of Households Per Capita Income and Households Per Capita Actual Consumption in the 141 Villages Studied

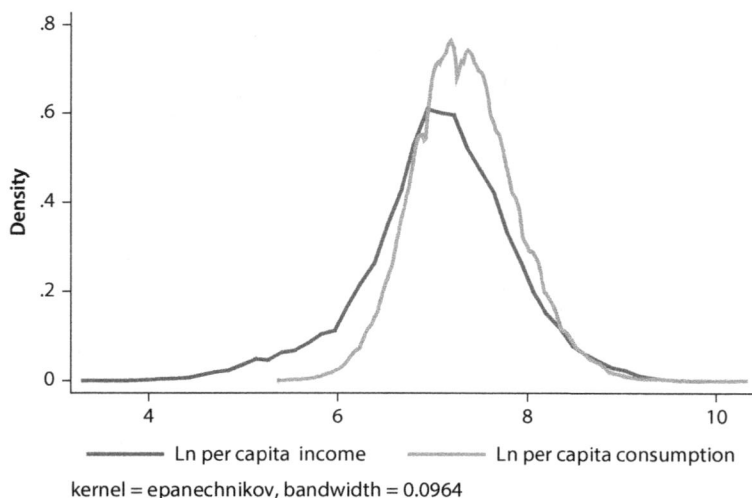

kernel = epanechnikov, bandwidth = 0.0964

Source: Calculated by the authors, out of the baseline survey of the 1,000 Poorest Villages Intervention.

rural Egypt. The Gini coefficient amounted to 29.4 in the study villages; which is less than the national Gini coefficient 31.1, but larger than the Gini coefficient of all rural Egypt (22.4) (see table 4.3).

Hence, these results indicate that—regardless of the measure of inequality used—the study villages suffer a level of inequality comparable to the overall level in total Egypt (although slightly lower in general), but certainly inequality in these villages is higher than in total rural Egypt.

The Lorenz curve in figure 4.5 also emphasizes the differences between the national and total rural Egypt per capita consumption trends compared to the 141 villages. While 60 percent of the population in the 141 villages consumes only 39 percent of the total consumption, the corresponding percentages were 55 percent, 50 percent for total rural Egypt and all Egypt, respectively.

Among the governorates represented in the baseline study, Assiut has the highest Gini coefficient (31.3), for example highest level of inequality among the study villages, while Behera has the lowest (22.6), followed by Menia (see figure 4.6). Figure 4.7 provides 95 percent confidence intervals for the Gini coefficient per village in the sample.

Figure 4.8 shows a slight negative relationship between inequality and the level of poverty in the village, while figure 4.9 shows a slight positive relationship between inequality and the level of ultra/extreme poverty in the village.

Table 4.3 Inequality Measures from Egypt Households Income, Expenditure and Consumption Survey in 2008/09 and in the Study Villages

	HIECS data 2008/09*		
Inequality measure	Egypt	Rural Egypt	141 study villages**
Ratio of the 80th percentile to the 20th percentile	4.5	3.1	3.9
Percent consumption share of the first quintile in total consumption	9	11	9.8
Gini Coefficient	31.1	22.4	29.4

Source: (*) HIECS 2008/2009 Report, by Central Agency for Public Mobilization and Statistics (CAPMAS); (**) Calculated by the authors.

Figure 4.5 Per Capita Consumption Lorenz Curve

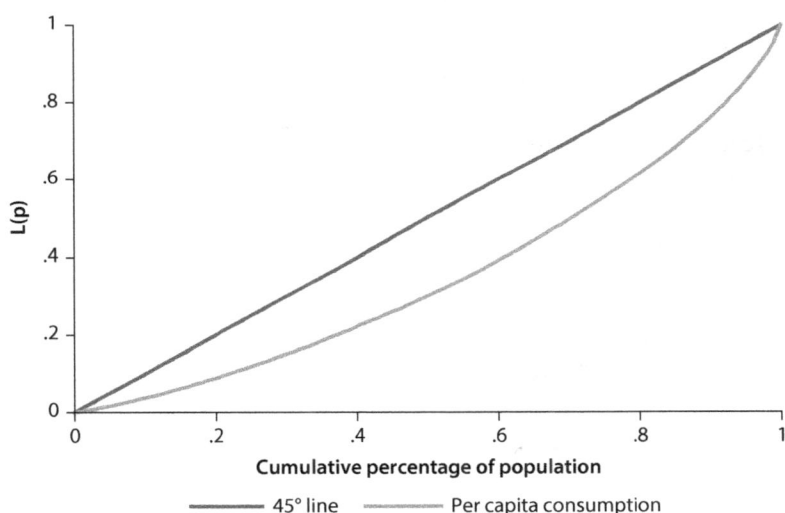

Source: Calculated by the authors, out of the baseline survey of the 1,000 Poorest Villages Intervention.

Figure 4.6 95 percent Confidence Interval for Gini Coefficient Per Governorate

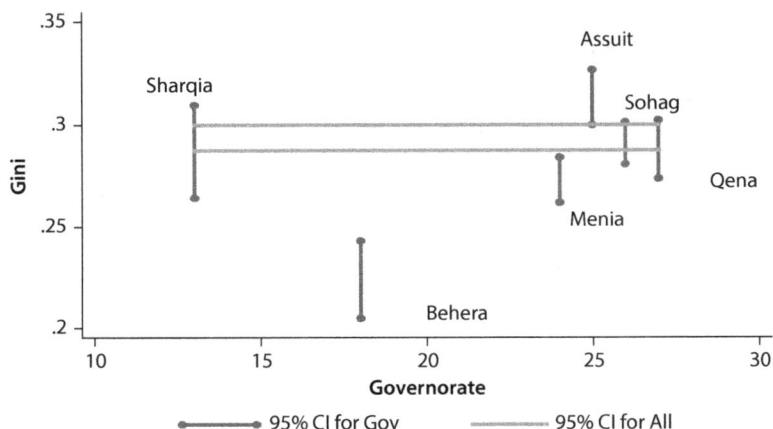

Source: Calculated by the Authors, out of the baseline survey of the 1,000 Poorest Villages Intervention.

Inside Inequality in the Arab Republic of Egypt • http://dx.doi.org/10.1596/978-1-4648-0198-3

Figure 4.7 95 percent Confidence Interval for Gini Coefficient Per Village

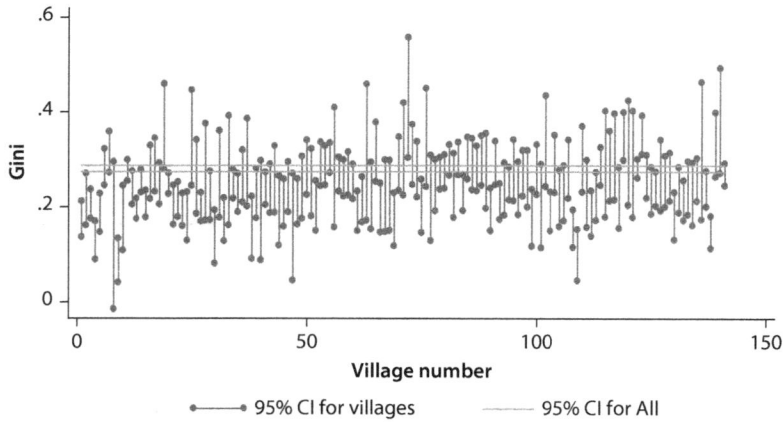

Source: Calculated by the Authors, out of the baseline survey of the 1,000 Poorest Villages Intervention.

Figure 4.8 Gini Coefficient by Percentage of Poor Household in Study Villages

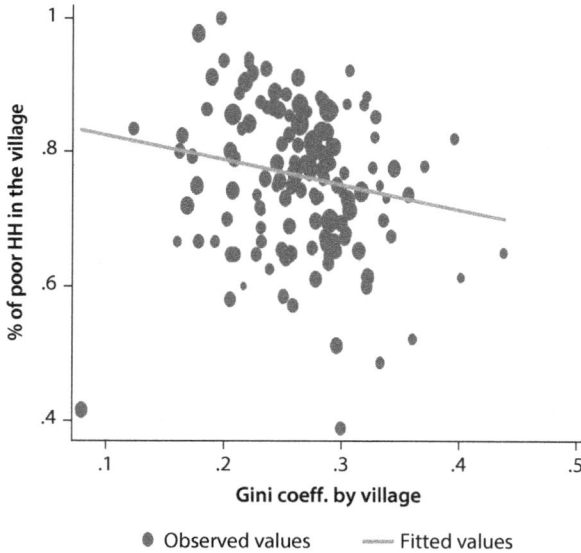

Source: Calculated by the authors, out of the baseline survey of the 1,000 Poorest Villages Intervention.
Note: HH = household.

Excluding outlier villages from the two graphs did not result in any changes in these two detected relationships/patterns between poverty and ultra poverty on the one hand and the Gini coefficient on the other.

Figure 4.9 Gini Coefficient by Percentage of Ultra-Poor Household in Study Villages

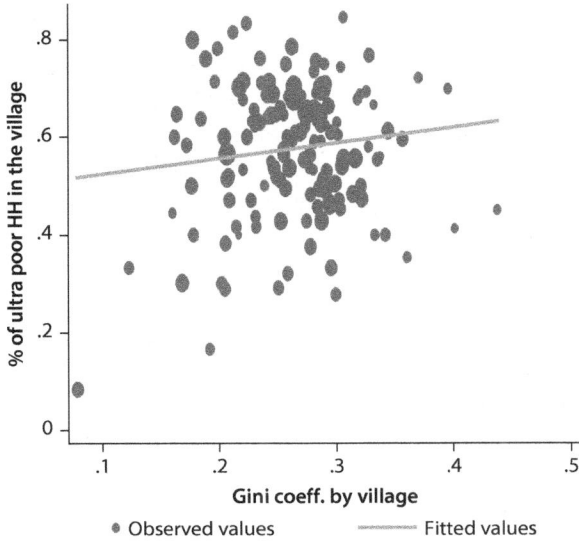

Source: Calculated by the authors, out of the baseline survey of the 1,000 Poorest Villages Intervention.
Note: HH = household.

The Conceptual Framework and Methodology

Determinants of poverty as well as the determinants of inequality reflect the human capital theory and the production theory (Wan and Zhou 2004). As seen in figure 4.10 inequality can be explained by the ability to generate income within

Figure 4.10 Determinants of Income/Consumption Inequality

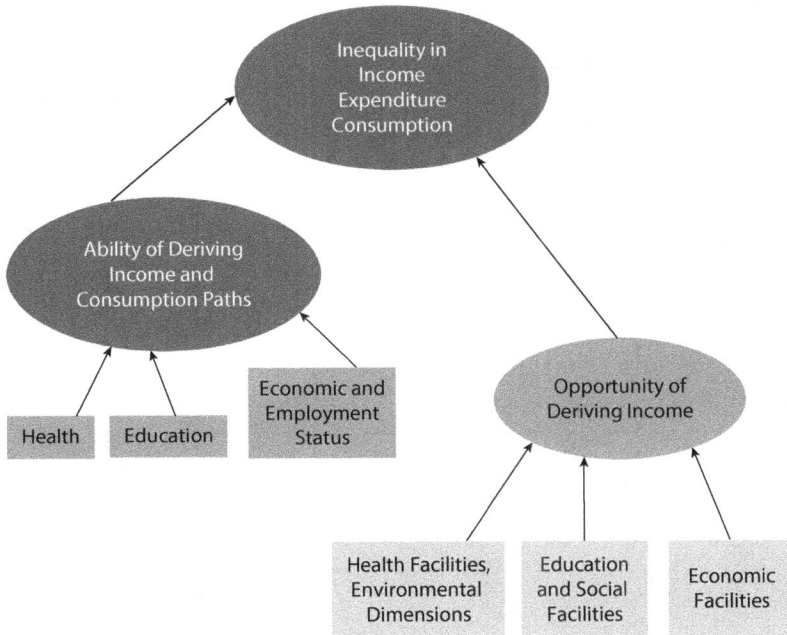

the household, summarized by health, education, employment, and economic status. These statuses can be measured by different variables or even proxies. While the previous variables contribute to differences in consumption from one household to another (within village inequality), the differences in consumption distribution from one village to another can be explained by the availability of certain facilities/services that provide better circumstances for health, education, and employment, such as the presence of health facilities, schools, factories, paved roads, and even the distance to main cities where more facilities are available, which provide diverse job opportunities and hence, income to the village residents.

To investigate the determinants of household poverty (measured by the natural logarithm of household actual per capita consumption) and, at the same time, to assess the contribution of each determinant to the resulting inequality between-households, regression-based inequality decomposition was applied to all 10,568 households in the 141 villages of the study. For the purpose of studying the determinants of within-villages inequality, aggregated data at the village level were used and weighted. Least squares regression was applied to the Gini coefficient data of the 141 villages.

Regression-based Inequality Decomposition

The Oaxaca-Blinder methodology is one of the pioneer approaches in inequality decomposition. However, it is criticized for considering only the differences between the means of the outcomes and not other distribution characteristics such as dispersion (Wang 2002; Jenkins and Van Kerm 2008). An alternative technique that has been used in inequality decomposition is the quantile regression that uses more characteristics of the conditional distribution (median, upper, and lower quartiles, or different percentiles).

The regression-based inequality decomposition has recently attracted many researchers to identify the contribution of different income/consumption sources to inequality (Murdoc and Sicular 2002; Cowell and Fiorio 2009; Brewer et al. 2010; Baye et al. 2011). It has also been used for decomposing income inequality by factor components using household level data (Wan 2004; Wan and Zhou 2005; Devicienti 2008; Brewer et.al. 2010; Nashold 2010).

This section is concerned with decomposing per capita consumption and inequality simultaneously by different factors going beyond decomposing by subpopulation groups. We aimed to quantify the direct role of different factors separately, while controlling for other variables that represent both household and village characteristics.

We applied the regression-based decomposition that was introduced by Shorrocks (1983, 1982), was extended by Fields in 2003, and, finally developed in STATA by Fiorio and Jenkins in 2007. Shorrock's (1982) technique is based on a decomposition rule for which inequality in the concerned variable across observations can be expressed as the sum of inequality contributions from each of the factor components. He also showed that the technique is independent of the inequality index; however, it can be written as a function of the coefficient of variation (equation 3).

Fields (2003) used the decomposition rules of Shorrock (1982) to propose a very similar approach based on regression technique, which allows one to assess the weight of different characteristics in explaining the level of inequality. This decomposition provides the variable's percentage contribution to the overall inequality, and hence the importance of the factors can be ranked for setting priorities among proposed policies.

The method is based on the regression equation as follows:[10]

$$\ln(y) = \alpha + \beta X + \varepsilon \tag{1}$$

where y is a $n \times 1$ vector of income/expenditure/consumption; X is an $n \times (K + 1)$ matrix of explanatory variables that reflect two groups of variables: the first group measures the health, education, and the economic and employment status within the household and the second group reflects the village differences; β is a $(K + 1) \times 1$ vector of coefficients and ε is a $n \times 1$ vector of residuals. The relative contribution is:

$$s_k = \frac{\text{cov}(\breve{\beta}_k x_k, y)}{\sigma_y^2} = \frac{\breve{\beta}_k \sigma_{x_k} \rho(x_k, y)}{\sigma_y} \tag{2}$$

$$s_k = \rho(\breve{\beta}_k x_k, y) \frac{\mu_{\breve{\beta}_k x_k}}{\mu_y} \frac{CV(\breve{\beta}_k x_k)}{CV(y)} \tag{3}$$

$$s_\varepsilon = 1 - R^2 \tag{4}$$

$$\sum_{k=1}^{K} s_k = R^2 \tag{5}$$

Applying the conceptual framework in figure 4.10 to the data of the 141 poorest villages we attempted to examine the importance and the impact of the following variables on the consumption inequality:

Head of household characteristics: These are age, sex, educational attainment, and employment status, which was grouped as not working, working in government/public sector, working in the private sector in an establishment, working in the private sector outside an establishment in nonagriculture activity, and, finally, working in the private sector outside an establishment in agriculture.

Household members characteristics: The impact of the ratio of children to household size was tested as well as the presence of internal and/or external migrants among household members, which may be an income source to the family.[11] We also considered the ratio of working individuals[12] within the household to the household size, and the number of permanent workers to total workers in the household. The presence of household members suffering chronic diseases, and handicapped individuals within the household were used as health indicators for ability to work. For economic status we used ownership of land, tractors or truck, or cattle, since in rural Egypt these physical capital variables help in generating income to the household in addition to wages (Wan and Zhou 2004).

Village characteristics: Village dummies and distance to the nearest urban center/town and distance to the capital city of the governorate were used to reflect the villages' differences.

Gini Coefficient Regression

While regression-based techniques use the household level characteristics in addition to the village characteristics in identifying the inequality determinants between households, a second methodology adopted in the analysis was regressing Gini coefficients of the villages on the villages and aggregated household characteristics (Litchfield 1999). For this purpose, we used least square regression weighted by the inverse of the coefficient standard error.

The variables used in this regression reflect the differences between the villages in the provision of health and educational services, along with economic facilities, such as the presence of clinics, high schools, paved roads, factories, post offices, banks, and agriculture land.

In addition to these variables, aggregated household characteristics were included, such as average size of household, percentage of households headed by males, percentage of individuals with chronic disease and/or disability within the village, percentage of illiterate individuals, and individuals with intermediate education. The percentage of workers among residents was considered in addition to the ratio of permanent workers to total workers. Finally, population density and the village's distance to the nearest urban center/town and distance to the capital city of the governorate were investigated as potential sources of the Gini coefficient's variation between villages.

Results

Table 4.4 summarizes the simultaneous effects of different determinants on inequality and poverty level of the household measured by the natural logarithm of per capita actual consumption. By applying the regression-based method to household level data, about 37.3 percent of the inequality between households can be explained by the factors included in the model. By far, the contribution of household characteristics outweighed the corresponding contribution of the characteristics of the villages in explaining inequality between households; 31 percent were strictly due to household characteristics while only 6.3 percent were due to the differences between villages where these households reside.

Concerning the latter, the distance from the village to the nearest town/urban center and the size of agricultural land in the village as well as the nonexistence of factories within one hour from the village were all insignificant factors in this regard. However, the first factor—the distance from the village to the nearest town/urban center—represents 1.6 percent of total inequality; that is, a village closer to an urban center may have easier access to a more diversified job market with variable returns to jobs, thus contributing to widening of the consumption gaps (increasing inequality) compared to the closed job market in the village

Table 4.4 Determinants of Ln Household Per Capita Consumption and Regression-Based Decomposition of Inequality by Factor Component

Ln household per capita consumption	Coefficient	$P > \lvert t \rvert$	Factor contribution to inequality[a]
Residual			62.6828
Household head (HH) characteristics			5.2045
Reference: Age of HH≥55 years			
Age of HH <25	0.0803	0.0440**	0.0587
Age of HH 25–34	0.0794	0.000***	0.0629
Age of HH 35–44	0.0154	0.3010	−0.1877
Age of HH 45–54	−0.0330	0.009***	0.1090
Reference: Female HH			
Male HH	−0.0761	0.000***	0.1908
Reference: Illiterate HH			
Less than primary and reads or writes	0.0360	0.004***	−0.0313
Primary	0.0656	0.002***	−0.0743
Preparatory	0.1134	0.000***	0.0459
Secondary/intermediate	0.2002	0.000***	0.9273
Above intermediate	0.2467	0.000***	0.1129
University +	0.4179	0.000***	2.6945
Reference: Not working HH			
Government/public sector	−0.1374	0.000***	−0.3578
Private in establishment	0.0157	0.4890	0.0671
Private outside establishment nonagriculture	−0.0713	0.000***	0.0630
Private out of establishment in agriculture	−0.1583	0.000***	1.5235
Assets: Ownership of			2.5914
Agriculture machines	0.0579	0.0070***	0.2142
Agriculture land	0.1455	0.000***	2.2466
Sheep and cows	0.0047	0.6750	−0.0382
Truck	0.1285	0.000***	0.1688
Household members characteristics			23.1888
Disabled in HH	−0.1112	0.000***	0.4260
Chronic disease in HH	−0.03127	0.001***	−0.0288
# of workers/HH size	0.6413	0.000***	9.0089
# of Permanent workers/# of workers	0.12086	0.000***	1.5301
Ratio of children to HH size	−0.68014	0.000***	11.6777
HH has an external migrant	0.16238	0.000***	0.6222
HH has an internal migrant	0.02791	0.1420	−0.0473
Village characteristics			6.3327
Distance from Markaz<10 KM	0.26356	0.1290	1.6259
Agriculture land <3 million sq meter	−0.02346	0.8920	0.0342
Number of factories within 1 hour is zero[b]	−0.04444	0.7980	0.0025
Village dummies	Omitted		4.6701
Constant	7.7567		

Source: World Bank data.

a. A positive sign indicates a disequalizing effect (increasing inequality) while a negative sign implies an equalizing effect (reducing inequality).

b. Reference category is one or more factories within a distance of 1 hour.

*** $p<0.01$, ** $p<0.05$, * $p<0.1$.

with much less variability in returns to jobs. On the other hand, 4.7 percent of inequality is due to the remaining differences between villages.

Table 4.4 also shows the contributions of three distinct sets of household characteristics to poverty and inequality in the 141 villages. The characteristics of the head of the household—although significant—contributed to only 5.2 percent of inequality. The least in terms of contribution to inequality were the age and sex of household head. Compared to households with older heads (age ≥55 years), household with a younger head (≤34 years old) experienced positive growth/reduced poverty in terms of increased per capita consumption until the head's age reaches 35–44 years. Controlling for all other factors in the model, when the age of the head of the household is 45–54 years, poverty is at its peak; probably due to the fact that by the time the head of the household reaches this age the household size also reaches a maximum (all children are born and not yet married, and the household may accommodate some elderly members as well).

Results showed that controlling for all the factors incorporated in the model, male-headed households were significantly in a worse situation compared to female-headed households in these villages as far as the level of household per capita consumption was concerned. However, it should be highlighted that female headed households comprised 7 percent of all households in the 141 villages; 90 percent of female headed households earned nonlabor income, and around two- thirds of them received pensions, remittances, or assistance (from government or other sources). In addition, female-headed households are usually smaller in size than male-headed households, which results in larger per capita consumption in the female-headed households even if the level of total consumption among the two types of households was initially the same.

Education attainment of the head of the household had a positive effect on per capita consumption in the household, and had the largest contribution to inequality among all characteristics of the head of household. The gap between households markedly increased when the head of household had a university degree (2.7 percent of inequality).

Working in the government or in the public sector had a negative effect on the growth of household consumption (that is increased poverty). This is understandable in the light of the extremely low remuneration received in government posts available in these poor communities. However, having a household head working (for others) outside an establishment, namely in agriculture, had the worst effect in terms of increasing household's poverty and also in terms of increasing inequality (1.5 percent). This latter group is known to suffer the most from the seasonality of employment.

They also suffer from a lack of social protection in terms of social insurance and health insurance, as well as unemployment and disability benefits. On the contrary, higher per capita consumption was related to households with non-working heads of households, which is due to having sources of income other than labor[13] from remittances, government pensions, or informal assistance. Also, households with heads working in private sector establishments share the same relatively better welfare status.

Physical capital (except ownership of sheep or cows) had a significant positive impact on deriving income and hence, consumption; in particular the possession of agricultural land widened the gap between households significantly and contributed to about 2.2 percent of explained inequality.

Most of the inequality that could be explained was due to the characteristics of the members of the households, mainly the ratio of children under the age of 15 to the total size of the household (11.7 percent), which contributed to a reduction in per capita consumption and a rise in inequality. The ratio of working household members came next with about 9 percent, and had a positive impact on consumption and contributed to increased inequality. A higher ratio of permanent workers among working household members increased the gap between households, but with a smaller impact on inequality (1.5 percent).

Having household members who are disabled and/or suffer from chronic disease had a significant negative impact on per capita consumption but did not contribute much to inequality. The same conclusion (but in the opposite direction) applied to having an external migrant among household members; it increased the per capita consumption of the household, but did not contribute much to inequality.

Table 4.5 summarizes the preceding results by listing the determinants that contributed simultaneously to increased/decreased inequality in the poorest villages by order of magnitude of their impact and also by whether each of these determinants had a positive or a negative effect on the household consumption/poverty.

Given the high correlation between households' per capita consumption within villages and the potential impact that this high correlation may have on the estimates of the parameters of the model and on the significance of these estimates, a generalized least square model using variance covariance matrix that allows standard errors to be intraclass correlated (by village) was applied (see the Annex). The results indicate a trivial change in the values of the estimates of the parameters related to the characteristics of the household's head and members between the generalized least square model and the regression-based inequality decomposition model. This trivial change in the values of the estimates was accompanied by a change in the level of the related P-values, however, with no change either in the directions of the effects of the parameters or in the overall significance of the estimates of these parameters. On the other hand, all three village-related characteristics used as proxies to access employment proved to be significant.

The weighted least squares regression based on the Gini coefficients of the villages confirmed some of the previous results (see table 4.6). The overall level of education in the village had a significant impact on the inequality within the villages; a higher ratio of highly educated residents increased the estimated Gini coefficient of the village. The infrastructure variables, such as having a paved road, or availability of different facilities, such as post office, clinic, bank, or high school, did not affect the inequality significantly.

Employment and the job market within the village were important factors in widening inequality. Smaller areas of agricultural land in the villages led to less inequality within the village (lower Gini coefficient) to the extent it led to lower

Table 4.5 Cross-Classification of the Determinants of Inequality and Poverty Ordered within Cells According to Contribution to Inequality

Ln HH consumption/capita	(+) Contribution (increasing inequality)	(−) Contribution (decreasing inequality)
(+) Coefficient (reducing poverty)	• More are employed among household members • Head of household attained secondary education or higher (especially university or higher) • Ownership of assets (especially agriculture land) • Closer distance to urban centers • More have permanent jobs among employed household members • Having external migrant among household members • Age of head of household is less than 35 years	• Some education
(−) Coefficient (increasing poverty)	• Higher fertility (ratio of children<15 years to household size) • Working in the private sector outside establishment in agriculture • Handicapped among household members • Male-headed households • Age of head of household is 45–55 years • Working in the private sector outside establishment not in agriculture	• Working in government or public sector • Chronic disease among household members

Source: World Bank data.
Note: HH = household head.

Table 4.6 Determinants of Inequality Using Gini Coefficients

Variables	Coefficient (standard errors in parentheses)
Fraction of male-headed households	−0.1760** (0.0712)
Average household size	−0.0037 (0.0097)
Fraction of internal migrants of the residents	−0.2000 (0.2080)
Fraction of external migrants of the residents	0.1150 (0.1910)
Fraction of chronic diseased individuals in the village	−0.0591 (0.1480)
Fraction of handicapped individuals in the village	0.5240 (0.3410)

table continues next page

Table 4.6 Determinants of Inequality Using Gini Coefficients (continued)

Variables	Coefficient (standard errors in parentheses)
No. of permanent workers/no. of workers	0.0414*
	(0.0248)
Fraction of workers of the residents	−0.0701
	(0.0725)
Fraction of individuals (age 10+) with university degree	0.3590**
	(0.1660)
Agriculture land in the village <3 millions m^2	−0.0411***
	(0.0102)
Distance to Markaz <10 KM	0.0050
	(0.0077)
Population density	5.5870**
	(2.248)
Village has high school	0.0088
	(0.0076)
Number of factories within 1 hour is zero[a]	−0.0138***
	(0.0084)
Constant	0.4190***
	(0.0803)
Observations	141
R^2	0.3650
Adjusted R^2	0.2940
P-Value	0.0000

Source: World Bank data.
a. Reference category is one or more factories within a distance of 1 hour.
***$p<0.01$, ** $p<0.05$, * $p<0.1$.

likelihood of landownership on the one hand and, also, less likelihood of working for others in agriculture; both correlates with lower inequality within village as indicated by the results of the household-level analysis.

On the other hand, the presence of factories nearby the village may provide "stable, permanent" jobs for some residents and therefore more inequality since a higher ratio of permanent workers increased the inequality as well. Finally, higher population density increased the Gini coefficient, and a higher percentage of households within the village that are headed by a male were negatively correlated to inequality.

Migration, whether internal or external, did not contribute to inequality within villages. It must be mentioned that causality between inequality and migration cannot be explained using the OLS, since high inequality within a village may be a cause to migrate or a result of inflows of remittances to the village.

Discussion and Policy Recommendations

Poverty and inequality motivated the Egyptian revolution of the 25th of January. Not surprisingly, social justice, fighting poverty, and reducing inequality have become top priorities on the agendas of the new Egyptian governments. Targeting the poor in general, and geographic targeting of the poorest communities in particular, is a necessary first step in developing strategic plans to initiate a more equitable and inclusive growth.

Unlike the situation at the national level where poverty is generally shallow, poverty in the poorest villages is rather deep. These villages suffer from both high levels of poverty and high levels of extreme poverty. In turn, this situation correlates with higher levels of inequality than the average in rural Egypt. Understanding the determinants of household poverty and inequality in the poorest villages should highlight and prioritize public policies that must be adopted.

Providing work opportunities in the government or the public sector would reduce inequality; however, it would also have a negative impact on household poverty status and lead to increased overall poverty in the light of the very low wages provided for government employees.

The results suggest that in the context of Egypt's poorest villages, some of the most significant factors conducive to increased inequality—such as higher employment and higher education—are the same standard objectives of pro-poor poverty reduction strategies. Hence, pro-poor growth accompanied by increased inequality is a legitimate goal that should be pursued. Policies adopted to achieve this goal must also encompass providing incentives to promote investments in areas that are geographically nearby these villages to avail them of more and better jobs in private sector establishments.

Although very high, poverty levels in the poorest villages seem to be, at least relatively, contained through remittances received from household members working abroad. The development and implementation of special vocational and skill-enhancement programs that qualify young people in poor villages to meet the demand in the labor markets in other countries in the region, and fostering bilateral agreements with the governments of these countries to receive legal labor migration may also be a promising venue that would benefit those young people and their households at home. Furthermore, a serious consideration of increasing access of households in these villages to ownership of agriculture land and/or equipment—through access to credit or other interventions—will also result in reduced poverty and increased inequality.

In the context of these poorest villages, ensuring some education, even if it does not conclude in completing basic education, remains one main key factor in order to fight extreme poverty while reducing inequality. However, ensuring extended years of education beyond just the basic mandatory stage not only increases the supply of skilled labor but also pays off as it seems to provide diversified opportunities to break out of poverty.

Annex

Determinants of Ln Household Per Capita Consumption Using Generalized Least Squares Regression Model

Ln household per capita consumption	Coefficient	P>|t|	% Distribution
Household head (HH) characteristics			
Reference: Age of HH≥55 years			25.9
Age of HH <25	0.0803*	0.0990	1.1
Age of HH 25–34	0.0795***	0.0030	16.1
Age of HH 35–44	0.0154	0.5470	28.9
Age of HH 45–54	−0.0330*	0.0670	28
			100%
Reference: Female HH			7.3
Male HH	−0.0761***	0.0010	92.7
			100%
Reference: Illiterate HH			49.1
Less than primary and reads or writes	0.0360*	0.0640	14.8
Primary	0.0656**	0.0500	4.4
Preparatory	0.1134***	0.0000	3.2
Secondary/intermediate	0.2002***	0.0000	20.8
Above intermediate	0.2467***	0.0000	1.7
University +	0.4179***	0.000	6.2
			100%
Reference: Not working			13.7
Government/public sector	−0.1374***	0.0000	19.3
Private in establishment	0.0158	0.6590	6.9
Private outside establishment nonagriculture.	−0.0713***	0.0050	26.4
Private out of establishment in agriculture.	−0.1583***	0.0000	33.7
			100%
Assets: Ownership of			
Agriculture machines	0.0579*	0.0640	4.4
Agriculture land	0.1455	0.0000	25.7
Sheep and cows	−0.0047	0.749	23.6
Truck	0.1285	0.0020	1.3
Household members characteristics			
Disabled in HH	−0.1112***	0.0000	7.6
Chronic disease in HH	−0.0313**	0.0380	24.9
# of workers/HH size	0.6413***	0.0000	—
# of permanent workers/# of workers	0.1209***	0.0000	—
Ratio of children to HH size	−0.6801***	0.0000	—
HH has an external migrant	0.1624***	0.0000	7.1
HH has an internal migrant	0.0279	0.3100	5.5
Village characteristics			
Distance from Markaz<10 KM	0.2636***	0.0000	—
Agriculture land <3 million sq meter	−0.0235**	0.0230	—
Number of factories within 1 hour is zero[a]	−0.0444***	0.0000	—

table continues next page

Determinants of Ln Household Per Capita Consumption Using Generalized Least Squares Regression Model *(continued)*

Ln household per capita consumption	Coefficient	P>|t|	% Distribution
Village dummies	Omitted	—	—
Observations		10,567	
R^2		0.3732	
Constant	7.1024		

Source: Calculated by the authors.
Note: *** *p*<0.01, ** *p*<0.05, * *p*<0.1.
The GLS model depends on variance covariance matrix that allows standard errors to be intraclass (by village) correlated.
a. Reference category is one or more factories in a distance of one hour.

Also, expanding the government social safety network beyond female-headed households to target and cater toward the needs of households that suffer extreme poverty in these villages is imperative. Increased poverty combined with increased inequality seem to be the result of the household having disabled members, large number of children, or heads who work as agriculture laborers, or simply work outside of establishments. These households could be targeted for social assistance, social protection schemes, vocational training programs, education and health care support for children in the household (after ensuring provision of quality education and health care services in these villages). Efficient targeting within the poorest villages accompanied by proper interventions should contribute to enhancing households' status and to reducing inequality.

Notes

1. Nonmonetary poverty as measured by the multidimensional poverty index (MPI) highlights the prevalence of deprivations related to health, education, and decent housing conditions. Hence, it reflects a new dimension of poverty by focusing on persons whose resources are so limited as to exclude them from the minimum acceptable way of life.

2. Other indicators are used to measure different levels of the poverty lines: The food poverty line, which expresses the minimum required income, expenditure, or consumption to cover the basic human nutrition needs, and the upper poverty line. Both the lower and upper poverty lines have the same minimum food needs component. The lower poverty line calculates the nonfood needs by using the lower bound of nonfood poverty line, while the upper poverty line uses the upper bound of nonfood poverty line to define the poor.

3. The Gini coefficient is bounded between zero and one, with zero indicating absolute equality and one indicating absolute inequality. It measures the area between the equality line (every x population percentile receives exactly x share of total consumption) and the actual consumption share of cumulative population distribution. The Gini coefficient is especially sensitive to changes in inequality in the middle of the equivalent consumption distribution.

4. It is a measure of inequality that is insensitive to outliers either in the very top or very bottom tail of the consumption distribution. However, quintile ratios do not reflect what happens in other parts of the distribution.

5. The choice of the 1,000 poorest villages was based on Egypt's 2006 poverty map. The World Bank methodology of the poverty map was applied to the data of the 2006 census in Egypt together with the data of the Households Income, Expenditure and Consumption Survey (HIECS) of 2004/05.

6. The Central Agency for Public Mobilization and Statistics (CAPMAS) accessed the 2006 census records relevant to the study villages for the actual sample selection based on the stratification criteria described above and using systematic random selection within identified strata. Field validation of the selected sample was conducted prior to data collection.

7. Actual household consumption includes consumption of goods and services that were obtained from the market and home produced goods. Rents were imputed for households who owned houses, using median rent per room, which is different from the methodology in the HIECS. Imputations were also adopted for per capita expenditure on electricity, water, and sanitation of households who reported the availability of services but did not report expenditure for it.

8. "Poor by Design, Vulnerable at Best: Findings of the Baseline Survey" M&E System of Phase I of the GoE initiative to develop the poorest 1,000 villages, 2010.

9. The mean distance separating the population from the poverty line deflated by the poverty line.

10. See Nashold, 2010

11. Adams (1989) showed that remittances had negative impact on the income inequality in rural Egypt.

12. Questionnaire does not specify the employment status according to waged or nonwaged.

13. Around 88 percent of nonworking heads of households received nonlabor income in the reference year compared to around 14 percent of working heads of households.

References

Adams Jr., R. H. 1989. "Worker Remittances an Inequality in Rural Egypt." *Economic Development and Cultural Change* 38, (1): 45–71.

Baye, F. M., and Epo, B. N. 2011. "Inequality Decomposition by Regressed-Income Sources in Cameroon." *Special IARIW-SSA Conference on Measuring National Income, Wealth, Poverty, and Inequality in African Countries.* Cape Town, South Africa.

Devicienti, F. 2008. "Shapley-Value Decompositions of Changes in Wage Distributions: A Note." LABORatorio R. Revelli Working Papers Series 80, LABORatorio R. Revelli, Centre for Employment Studies, Italy.

El-Laithy, H. 2009. "Complete and Partial Analysis of Pro-Poor Growth in Egypt 2000–2008." Workshop paper PO_09_01, Economic Research Forum, Cairo, Egypt.

El-Laithy, H., El-Tawila, S., Armanios, D., Saad, M., Bayoumi, D., Fekry, A., Ali, E., Refaat, I., and Youssef, B. 2010. "Monitoring and Evaluation System of the Government Initiative to Develop the Poorest 1000 Villages, Poor by Design, Vulnerable at Best: Findings of the Baseline Assessment in the 151 Villages of Phase-I of the Initiative." Information and Decision Support Center, Social Contract Center, and Research Monitoring& Governance Unit. Draft Report.

Fiorio, C. V., and P. S. Jenkins. 2003. "Regression-based Inequality Decomposition Following Fields." Institute for Social & Economic Research (ISER)—University of Essex, Colchester.

———. 2007. "Regression-based Inequality Decomposition Following Fields 2003." Presentation at Institute for Social & Economic Research (ISER)—University of Essex, September 2007. www.stata.com/meeting/13uk/fiorio_ineqrbd_UKSUG07.pdf.

Fiorio, C. V., and F. A. Cowell. 2009. "Inequality Decomposition—A Reconciliation." Suntory and Toyota International Centres for Economics and Related Disciplines, LSE.

Jenkins, S., and P. Van Kerm. 2008. "The Measurement of Economic Inequality." Prepared for the Oxford Handbook on Economic Inequality edited by Brian Nolan, Wiermer Salverda and Tim Smeeding.

Kimhi, A. 2007. "Regression-Based Inequality Decomposition: A Critical Review and Application to Farm-Household Income Data." The Center for Agricultural Economic Research, the Department of Agricultural Economics and Management; the Hebrew University of Jerusalem.

Litchfield, J. A. 1999. Inequality Methods and Tools, Text for World Bank's site on Inequality, Poverty and Socio-economic Performance. http://www.worldbank.org.

Ministry of Economic Development, Social and Economic Development Group. 2007. "Arab Republic of Egypt Poverty Assessment Report." Middle East and North Africa Region, World Bank, Washington, DC.

Morduch, J., and T. Sicular. 2002. "Rethinking Inequality Decomposition, with Evidence from Rural China." *The Economic Journal, Royal Economic Society*, 93–106.

Naschold, F. 2009. "Microeconomic Determinants of Income Inequality in Rural Pakistan." *Journal of Development Studies* 45 (5): 746–68.

Social Contract Center, Information and Decision Support Center. 2009. Phase I: 151 Villages, Cairo, Egypt.

Shorrocks, A. F. 1982. "Inequality Decomposition by Factor Components." *Econometrica* 50 (1): 193–211.

———. 1984. "Inequality Decomposition by Population Subgroups." *Econometrica* 52 (6): 1369–85.

Wan, G. H. 2002. "Regression-based Inequality Decomposition." Discussion Paper No. 101, World Institute for Development Economics WIDER, Helsinki.

———. 2004. "Accounting for Income Inequality in Rural China: A Regression-based Approach." *Journal of Comparative Economics* 32(2), 348–63.

Wan, G. H., and Z. Zhou. 2004. "Income Inequality in Rural China." Research Paper No. 51, World Institute For Development Economics Research WIDER, Helsinki.

———. 2005. "Income Inequality in Rural China: Regression-based Decomposition Using Household Data." *Review of Development Economics* 9 (1): 107–20.

World Bank. 2007. "Arab Republic of Egypt A Poverty Assessment Update." Report No. 39885—EG Joint report with the Ministry of Economic Development, Egypt.

green press
INITIATIVE